COMES THE AWAKENING

Realizing the Divine Nature Of Who You Are

Lia Shapiro

A PLEIADIAN BOOK

Star Street Press
★
Washington D.C.

Comes The Awakening
Realizing the Divine Nature of Who You Are

Copyright © 2000 Lia Langnas Shapiro

Library of Congress Control Number 00 133479

Star Street Press
420 7th Street NW
Suite 1013
Washington, DC 20004
1-800-587-9178
www.starstreetpress.com

Cover & Book Design by Lia Shapiro

Cataloging In Publication Data

Shapiro, Lia
    Comes the Awakening : realizing the divine
nature of who you are / Lia Shapiro. -- 1st ed.
    p. cm. ∂ 54 p.
    Includes index.
    ISBN: 0-9701128-5-8

    1. New Age movement. 2. Self-actualization
(Psychology) 3. Metaphysics 4. Spiritual Life.
5. Pleiades--Religious aspects. I. Title.

BP605.N48S53 2000   299.93
                        QBI00-500035

Manufactured in the United States of America

Printed on acid free paper

FIRST EDITION

10 9 8 7 6 5 4 3 2 1

THANK YOU

I offer thanks to the Spirit within, the Pleiadians who exist as a part of me, and Spirit/God beyond which is a part of us all and connects us.

Thank you dear family for your love, your patience and your belief in me. My husband, Don Shapiro for his never ending encouragement, unlimited love and help whenever I needed it, which was often! My dearest daughter, Kristin Buzzelli, for her loving support, sound advice and expert editing on finding all those last minute mistakes. My son, Tom Kendle, for being a Light and for helping to direct me. My son, Ryan Kendle, for all his patient hours of listening to me and for his invaluable and thoughtful advice. My brother, Robert Langnas, because we have the same genes and he understands.

Thank you friends and beings for your love and your support. In one way or another, each of you has contributed to this endeavor by your inspirational force and presence. We are all one and I love you!

Lee Carroll...Anthony D. Davis...Kevin Davis
Phil Erickson...Pelle Handén
Ronna Herman...Peter Henochsberg
Phil Gruber...Lexxus Lashley
Louis Martin...Shekego Masuda...Magoria
René Muller...Brian E. Paulson
Margaret Pinyan...Glenn Pruit
James "Gentleheart"Taylor
Sanaya Roman...John A. Spera
O'Ryin Swanson

Table of Contents

Awareness brings realization.
Realization causes an awakening.
Awakening brings us to an
in-Lightened state.
In the Light, you will find your truth....
and finally you will know the power is within
you.

Chapter One

Lia's Awakening

Where do I begin to tell the story? Perhaps the story begins when I was born, or does it begin at the beginning of time? My soul streaks through time, so it is indeed difficult to pinpoint the precise moment with which it all started. The Pleiadians...oh yes, you want to know about the Pleiadians. Or do you want to know about Lia Shapiro? Are they one and the same? Yes, I believe so, although you might wonder how this could be.

I am Pleiadian at a higher level...in another realm. What does this mean? Well, you may have to read and absorb the information in this book to find out. If I try to tell you here, then I will end up channeling another chapter and you will not get to hear about the human aspect of who I am.

I am Lia Shapiro here, at this precise moment in time. I popped into the Earth reality in the year of 1949. Yes, this is correct if you calculate time as linear. Okay, so I have just given away my earthly age, but does it matter when my soul simply glides agelessly and effortlessly through time?

Yes, I had Earth parents, or is it only my perception that they were Earthlings? Nevertheless, my father was Jewish, and my mother a lovely, fair, blonde and blue- eyed creature. They gave birth to five assorted humanoids. We are all still thriving happily in this world, or as happily as humans can thrive.

My parents never did quite figure out what beliefs or religion we should be raised with. Although my father was Jewish, he was also a professed atheist. My mother was Southern Baptist, but because my father was Jewish she did not want to raise her children in her religion. She succeeded in getting us through the 50's and 60's without a religion, although, this was probably unheard of in America during those times. I didn't know a thing about the Bible, but I did know about spirituality. We were not taught the ways of religion, but taught about the power of our own spirit. While my mother did not teach religiosity or make us go to church, she did have a powerful belief in God.

I was a hippie. Yes, give peace a chance and all that. I was a true flower child, headband, beads, barefoot, bellbottom jeans and a Volkswagen painted in a dazzling profusion of colors. It was a time of protesting for some, but for me it was a time of spiritual awakening. Washington D.C. was my home, so you could usually find me at the Washington Monument whenever something exciting was happening. The masses converged upon the city as one. Music and marijuana smoke mingled and drifted through the air, while protest singers often sang out loud and clear. I loved meandering through the multitudes, as the whole scene exuded a certain energy full of peace, power and purpose. Or so it seemed.

It was the *energy* of those times that stirred my soul and started an awakening deep within me. Without any formal or mandatory religious training, I had been free to find my own way. I sought out spiritual teachings, although I was not a follower of any particular teaching. Instead, I had experienced my own vision, going within it to find my own truths.

It was within a beautiful, heavenly, golden place that I found myself. I will pause here, to tell you there are really no earthly words to describe this profound and powerful experience, but I will try. Nevertheless, it was in this place that I felt and knew, and saw myself as a body of golden,

shimmering Light. By my side, there was a fellow
Light Being. Beautifully, and together as soul
friends, we traveled layer by layer through the
Heavens. Immediately, I was ushered into a new
world in which I knew, but had not remembered.

When my vision first began, radiant beams
shone down on me like translucent gold pouring
from the sun. All at once, a choir of angelic voices
burst into the most extraordinary song, filling my
soul with sounds never before heard upon the face
of the Earth. It was more beautiful than anything
I can describe and more exquisite than anything I
have ever seen or experienced in this physical
world. It was a moment of spiritual bliss and true
ecstasy, when in the next shimmering moment I
saw the face of Jesus. He did not speak but I
heard him say, "See, this is where we go." He was
not the Jesus that the Bible has made of him, but
he was as we are. He had simply brought truths
from a higher realm...and they turned him into the
Son of God.

We are all Suns and originate in the Light! For
whatever reason, and for a moment in physical
Earth time, I experienced this Place of Light. I
cried and gasped for air as the forces of love and
joy, all at once, seemed to pour in through the top
of my head, consuming and filling me completely.
It was so much that it seemed to spill out of me
and I could not hold it all.

In this place of Light, I traversed the layers of the universe itself. Every step of the way, answers were given to me as I went higher and higher. Finally, reaching the top or so it seemed, I found that this is where God was. Oh, what a magnificent revelation! God was not outside of me, but inside, and at the very highest level of my being! Inside every creation in the universe, God is dwelling there. You are God. I am God. We are all God and God is us!

Regrettably, I did not remain in my vision, but came back to Earth with a thud. I fell in love, and yes, with a mortal being. It was then off to Iran for two years with my husband and his new job. Far away from America, my friends and family and feeling very isolated and alone, I had plenty of time to think, evolve and develop my soul.

I had two marriages and created three beautiful children between the years of 1968 and 1997. My husband of twenty-three years was a practical, logical kind of guy. He did not believe in visions or even in God for that matter. I soon decided that as long as I was in this world, I would have to set spiritual things aside and focus on the business at hand. Of course, that didn't last for too long. Everyone around me seemed to be having this *born again* experience. The last thing I needed was religion! My father-in-law was a Fundamentalist Baptist preacher and had turned my husband completely away from anything spiritual.

At this juncture in my life, I had slammed a lid on my spirituality, denying it for the sake of peace and harmony in my marriage. Then one day the inevitable happened. I had come to the end of myself and there was nothing left but spirit. We had lost a business, a home and had just had our third child. After having to make some major changes, moving from the West Coast to the East Coast, and the flail to financially survive, I had a major leap in my spirituality and got *born again*. At the time, I was so ill informed about religion that I did not realize I had become a *Born Again Christian*. This is the term used in the Bible, "For unless ye be born again, ye will not see the Kingdom of God."

I did not come by the way of Jesus. I didn't believe in Jesus or not in the Biblical sense anyway. I didn't believe in sin either, but I read the prayer in the booklet my sister had sent, just in case. That was the day I simply gave up. Yes, that's what I did. I said, "Okay, God, I give up," and I read the prayer twice just to make sure. I had no one to turn to but God, although I was not sure where God was; I only knew that I needed divine help.

That night, the presence of God overcame me completely. The walls that I had begun to build came tumbling down. I cried, so full of joy to feel the presence of something divine again. My eyes saw sparkles for the next three days as I kept blinking to see if the sparkling would go away. Finally, I went out into the throng of humanity again, but felt that everyone was looking at me, knowing that something tremendous had happened.

A peace had replaced the agitation in my soul. I didn't yell at my kids anymore. I didn't need to. I'd gone through a major, spiritual, evolutionary leap. At the time we were living temporarily in the guesthouse of my in-laws. It sat right smack and conviently in the middle of a Baptist youth camp. My in-laws, of course, were ecstatic at my conversion and equally happy to have me there. Immediately, they proceeded in giving me lessons in the Bible every day. I learned that I had become a Christian! How come I hadn't known this when it happened?

Finally, I could not escape my own spirituality. It came full force at me and I thought surely my husband would demand a divorce. I had become what his parents had forced on him as a child. My in-laws, sisters, friends, everyone around me, it seemed, had become a *Born Again Christian*. They were all eager to get me into church and to make sure I followed only the Bible. I not only read the entire Bible, but I studied it thoroughly, following and obeying its teachings, then proceeded to raise my children to believe it was the only way.

Eventually, my husband's job took us to Nairobi, Kenya. We spent three years in Africa. I had left the safety net of my church and my Christian friends. I now worked and lived in a strange new foreign community. Not only did I encounter many different kinds of people, but different beliefs as well. It seemed no matter who I talked to and what their religion was, we were all talking about the same thing whether it was called God, Allah or whatever.

My parents died while I was in Africa. They had divorced when I was a teenager and I had not been in contact with my father since. My mother told me he had died of colon cancer, and then she died of a heart attack...or maybe it was from heartbreak. She had continued to love him all those years...as I continue to love her now.

Out of Africa and back to America, I no longer attended church; nevertheless, I continued to raise my children with the secure feeling of having a God and a definite set of rules to go by...the Bible. Frequently, and often secretly throughout the years, I had thought about my vision and what it had all meant. Christian friends had tried to tell me it was of the Devil, but I knew in my heart that it was not. It had been a deep and profound experience that carried tremendous impact and affected my entire life. It was my very own soul that had experienced and awakened to the divine nature of who I was.

Off again, this time to Tokyo, Japan, an awesome city and totally alien, in the human sense of the word, of course. I could not read, write, communicate, nor understand anything of the language or the people. It was a turbulent time, but a time for profound and permanent changes within and outside of myself. I was still deeply religious, but Japan was definitely not a religious country, or religious in the way that Western civilization might recognize.

My husband traveled extensively all over Asia. My children were teenagers and happily finding new freedom in Tokyo, riding the subway anywhere they wanted. Japan is an extremely safe country with no worries or fears about allowing one's children to roam. And so it was that I either spent many hours alone or immersing myself into the Japanese culture by teaching English. Teaching English in Japan encompasses much more than simply teaching English. It involves a cultural exchange, which includes many topics of interests in the course of an English conversation.

One day the group topic turned to that of spiritual matters. I spoke enthusiastically and scribbled on the black board. I felt very excited about opening up this new spiritual realm to inquisitive Japanese minds. Later that afternoon, a pretty, sparkling, round faced Japanese woman approached me. With a mysterious smile on her face and a twinkle in her eye, she spoke in a broken

accent. "You are Light," she said. "You will have
a mission in the world."

Shigeko and I became friends, as she
encouraged me to listen to my heart and to write
down what I heard. Every day she would ask me
if I had started to write. Every day I would tell
her, no. She then began to tell me about UFO's,
aliens, pyramids and many other strange and
wondrous things. In the meantime, it seemed both
my husband and my religion were slipping away.
I started to have intense dreams, or visions, or
actual encounters during the remainder of my time
in Japan. Whether they existed in my current
reality, I still do not know. I only know that I saw
UFO's and beings, somewhere in time. Many were
my dreams and one night I only dreamt of
triangles. For the next two days, I doodled
triangles in all shapes, sizes and forms. I knew
that I had been *sleep learning.* I had learned the
power of triangles! I was learning so much, or
learning that which I had forgotten. One night
while drifting off to sleep, I heard a voice as if from
my deepest self. It was clear and the message was
important. I struggled, still halfway asleep, to find
a pen. From that night forward I always kept a
pen and paper on my night table. The messages
started to come, and so it was that I had started
to listen to my heart. Soon, I had scraps of paper
with all that I had written. The next time Shigeko
asked if I had started writing, I told her, "Yes."

One day it happened that I sat down at my computer, feeling extremely compelled to write something. I had always been a writer, but this was different. The words began to form in my mind, and as they did, I simply typed what I heard. I wrote pages, until finally I stopped to read what I had written. It was as if I were reading the information for the very first time.

In the meantime, my marriage of twenty-three years began to crumble. We left Japan and returned to the United States. I cannot begin to relate the horror of what was involved in the disintegration of a long marriage and of losing a family structure. This was not what I had wanted, but it seemed to be happening before my very eyes. Not only did I have to deal with the loss of my marriage, but with the loss of my religion, my children, and the shock of returning to America after finally adjusting to Japan and its ways.

I was alone and floundering. I felt destitute and miserable. I not only struggled emotionally but financially as well. I was no longer a Christian, but still I listened to my heart and wrote down the words that came to me. My world had fallen apart, yet I knew that I was entering a new world and there was a mission for me to fulfill. I also realized that I was only human at this level and that my struggle and sadness reflected that fact.

It is now that I do what I do, offering love, guidance, and wisdom from a higher realm because

I have gone through the valley of despair myself. I know what sadness and pain are all about. I know that life in this denser physical reality can become overwhelming and even a burden to our souls.

I had indeed plunged myself into a deep, dark valley, yet, I was able to see the sun shining at the top of the mountain. Keeping my eyes on the Light, while groping through the dark, I began to realize more and more that my external reality was indeed created from within me. In other words, I had to create what it was that I needed and wanted. Most of all I needed love, and so it was, that I set about creating my image of perfect love on this Earth.

Don came bursting into my world shortly after I started to focus intently on the issue of love. Not only did he eventually become my husband, but intuitively he seemed to know my purpose, even when I did not always know. By this time I had channeled an almost complete book. Still, I was determined to go down a path that would assure me of security and a life composed of the usual and normal kinds of things. I would not allow Don to help me in any way, even when I struggled so desperately. It is often that when we have a purpose or a certain mission, we can get lost in our struggle to survive this planet.

Survival. Isn't that what it's all about here? Most of us hurry and scurry to some job, forever bound, afraid and insecure to be who we really are. It takes a leap of faith to just stop and go after what we really love to do, or want to be, or need to express. Sometimes...it takes a crisis. As if enough hadn't already been heaped upon me, just as I was about to land the job of my dreams, I was stricken with meningitis. After four days in the hospital, and coming close to the edge of death, I assured my new employer that I would be better in a week.

I was not better in a week, but went through an agonizingly slow recovery over the next two years. In the months after the meningitis, I somehow had managed to get divorced and remarried. I had moved from Tokyo to Washington D.C. to Los Angeles, California. I had lost the ability to do some things, but gained remarkable new insights and abilities to do other things. I had married my dream man. Not only did I find a new and higher level of love with my new husband, but also, he recognized my purpose and mission.

Life here can be about many things. It is a slow and ever awakening process. Nothing is by accident, but all is for a reason. My reason for coming here was to evolve my own soul and to awaken in the process. My purpose for being here now is to love and to help others awaken.

It is with love that I bring you the Pleiadians. They are not God, but only exist at a higher level of who I am. God is at the highest. By going beyond myself, I have tuned into a higher, love based energy which is Pleiadian. The Pleiadians exist within me and outside of me, in another world or on another planet or dimension. They are more highly evolved than we are, yet they exist as a part of who we are. They are our future, yet it is possible they can traverse the universe and appear in our physical reality. More than likely, they work through the layers of our consciousness.

Time is not linear. We exist in the past, the present and the future all at once. I am human here, but in the far distant future, I am Pleiadian. It may be that you are Pleiadian, too. If so, then please, sit back, relax, and tune in. If you do not want to acknowledge such kinship, then please, I invite you to simply stay and learn with us. Take what you need, and discard what you don't need. The choice and the power is always yours.

Enter the Pleiadians

The beginning was long ago, but we remember, each of us, somewhere deep inside the layers of forgotten memory. Each and every one of us were there, not the body that we know now, but spirit. It was then when we came from far away to inhabit the earth, a new world, blue and green and beautiful it was.

The earth was inhabited at that time with other occupants, created long before we arrived by the same Creator that created all, but nevertheless, we were one and the same, as we are now - Creator and Creations. We are an extension of you going backward, and you are an extension of us going forward. In other words, we are an extension of each other going in opposite directions, and there is no ending to the beginning or the end. We, together, are the Alpha and the Omega, the Creation never ending, but going on and on and on, throughout all of time, forward and forever into the far reaches of endless eternity.

What we see now is only a point in time, a blip, a stop sign along the many paths that lead to the future, and it is indeed the future that is our concern. It is here that we pause to bring you a message, to bring Hope and Light that there is always a way if you look within yourselves. *You* are the ones we address ourselves to. *You* are the ones that know your names when called. Although you hesitate, not sure, not remembering; when you hear our voice, you will stop and incline your ear and ask, "Is it God?"

Call us what you will, although we have certainly been called God. The point is, we call you for a reason, and please believe this, we would not intrude unless it was urgent. We hope to reveal the intent of our purpose slowly throughout the course of our interaction with you. As you awaken and begin to remember, you will also remember why it is you chose to enter in at this particular point in time.

We would come to you personally, but there are many, and the time is short. Not that it would be impossible to accomplish this in ways that you do not comprehend yet, but understand this. Most of you do not recognize your purpose as of yet, but most of you *are* capable of reading. Reading is a common pastime upon planet Earth. Books are familiar. Unencumbered voices are not. We understand this.

Know that, however, this book came to be in your hands, it is indeed meant for *you*. There is a message contained in these pages and it would behoove you to continue reading. It is for you to find out the truth of yourself that is hidden beneath the layers, locked away deeply. If you listen carefully, we will help to unlock the secrets.

Shedding Light On the Human Condition

It was long ago, aeons and aeons, so far back in time that you will fail to grasp the meaning if you do not think carefully about it. It was before the great flood. It was before the Incas, Aztecs or Mayans. It was before anything you know of as events in time recorded as history. We are trying to impress upon you that what happened was so long ago that if you could imagine it, it would still come to you as incomprehensible. The events of those times happened before the beginning of the beginning of what you know as your Bible in the Western world. It was far back at this point that the world was a living, thriving, breathing, pulsating, blue and green sphere dangling like a jewel in space. It was as valuable as if it were composed of gold or diamonds, so valuable indeed that tremendous battles were fought in order to gain possession of the magnificent colored jewel.

Humans are interbred with many. You are not a descendent of the ape or monkey. The scientists have speculated but they have been wrong, very wrong. You are not, nor have you ever been left to your own to evolve according to some haphazard plan. You are a line of Light shooting like a star through space and time, evolving because of direct intervention. Call it divine intervention or call it what you will. The fact is, because of this unseen intervention, your growth and circumstances have been never ending, like the waves of the ocean, changing always, crashing upon foreign shores then back again, gentle and crashing on and on forever.

We must tell you that your evolvement has been due partly to genetic engineering performed by the best. Your so called implants are not pieces of metal or anything so crude as that. They are not necessarily tracking devices either. That way of thinking is only for the small minded. Broaden your mind, expand and remember what we have told you in other times. Implants are for your higher good. They only serve to finely tune what is already done. You may call it divine engineering, and we must say it is the finest.

If you ask for answers, you will certainly find them, although it may take a lifetime. A lifetime to you indeed seems very long, but it is in actuality just a blip in time. You may go through many phases, many belief systems. Perhaps even a devoutly religious phase, with no other thoughts but your sincere focus on God. That is not bad, as long as it is for the good of yourself and others.

You will gain more knowledge and as you do, your thoughts will begin to expand in ever widening circles. They will have a way of engulfing others. Some will come willingly into your circle and will know in their deepest selves that what you say is truth. Others will turn away and shun you, even hate you and call you cursed. You must turn away from them for they are not ready. You must not try to persuade them verbally. There is a higher way that we will discuss with you later. Nevertheless, those people and many like them will have to follow their own reality, just as you have done, and now it is your job to move on to higher realms.

You have read about our messages in other books and places. What you are reading now is not an imitation. It is not a copy. It is a new message for we have much to say and we will use many to accomplish our goals and purposes. Please be assured that our purpose is ultimately good. We want to be absolutely sure that you understand this.

We speak in the plural form, *we*, for we are small in number while at the same time we are many. When one speaks, we speak for all, for we are the Pleiadians of good and noble and divine purpose. It is our wish never to boast, but to only state the truth and the facts at all times. It is with much hope and our sincere desire and eagerness that you know in your deepest of hearts that what we tell you is the ultimate truth of all experience. That is why we come to you...that is why we give you this message. We hope that you receive it as a message of Hope...a message of Light...a message that will spur you on to greater and greater heights.

There are those of you that will recognize what we have to say as truth, and there are those that will not comprehend and will turn away. We are not concerned with the turn awayers. Our purpose is to speak to only you, and to speak again and again until you are permeated with our message. We want our message to get into your cells so much that you will not be able to stop thinking about it. It is then that you will start to remember. That is why you will not be able to put what we tell you out of your mind. The time is growing short and we must begin to activate that which you, yourself, know. The implants will help to accomplish that purpose.

We do wish at this time to apologize for any inconvenience. We realize our implants may cause some temporary problems, as well as interruptions, and much worry on your part. Some of you are not aware of the implants but others are, shall we say, those of you that are more finely tuned into their physical bodies. Yes, some of you know and understand your bodies well and it is you that will react, sometimes almost severely. It is with much regret and sorrow when we tell you that we never, never intend to hurt you, but only to help you. Please know this. Also, know that you must try to overcome the inconvenience, even the pain, that the implants sometimes may cause. Understand in your deepest self that it is necessary for the ultimate good and continual evolution of creation itself.

It is important that you remember, for you, dear one, are special, far more special than you can possibly know at this moment. Perhaps you are hearing this for the first time. Perhaps we have come to you before, in your dreams, in your thoughts, in another book. Do not be alarmed when we tell you this, but perhaps you have even seen or interacted with us in physical form! We do not intrude in a scary way, but always, we try to be mindful of the human condition. We do respect that.

We have an urgent message and we will come to you persistently in whatever way is deemed necessary for your current state. For many of you, we will work harmoniously within the layers of your conscious and unconscious mind. We will be perceived as perhaps nothing more than a dream, and even then, you may not even remember the dream, but be assured the message will be fully retained by you in some way or another. You are powerful and are able to receive that which we plant. Please know this and believe it, for it is what you agreed to long, long ago in another time and another place.

We are working with you as a unit. We are connected in a sense that you may not understand now, but slowly realization will come. We, the Pleiadians, are small in number at this point, but we are ever increasing day by day. Be assured that our band of so called *do-gooders* are growing.

We like to give a name to you for everything for we understand the necessity of human language, and so it is that we have chosen what we believe to be a humble but honorable name, the Pleiadians. It is a name with which you can easily identify with if you study the stars and study your legends. In choosing this name, our hope is that it will be easier for you to assimilate and accept rather than something which might be far too complex, intimidating, threatening or even overly mystical. We do try to be practical. Nevertheless, names are important because they radiate frequency. By now maybe you have heard of our small band of *do-gooders* and are even familiar with our mission. We believe it to be a mission of the utmost importance, and it can be complex, but not so complex that you do not know your part, for you are certainly half of the whole.

Without you our mission would be impossible, and without us, your lives and future lives would soon be extinguished. So, you can perhaps begin to see the urgency of what we come to tell you.

We are not from another galaxy in the dimension that you know. Reality is not that simple when you speak and think of such long distances. But, our reality is just as real and solid as your own, the only difference being that we can enter in and out at will according to our intentions. Trust us when we say we have found a way. As we have found a way, you also, will most certainly find it. Listen carefully, always. From now on, incline one ear and tune into a frequency that until now you have been oblivious to. If you do, we promise that only good things are in store for you. We honor you now and make a pledge at the very moment you read this. Inside of your deepest self, with all of your being, with all of your knowing, you will understand that it is you that we speak to.

Frequencies are such that you do not notice them. Your idea of frequency is perhaps the radio or television. These are simple frequencies, but they exist in your domain of reason and logic. Although you may not be familiar with frequencies, you do have some understanding that it is something technical and created by humans. Even if you know nothing at all about electronics, you do know that televisions and radios operate on some kind of frequency. Stop for a moment and consider another concept of frequencies. Now, listen carefully as we stress the word *All*. All life operates on frequency. Capitalize the word *All* and remember it. *All* realities operate on frequency. Frequency is the essence of life. Without it, life would not exist, therefore, when we speak of frequency, know from now on that it is as important as the air you breathe.

Frequencies are the rate of pulsations emanating from all life forms as well as all inanimate objects. Everything in your realm of existence pulsates with a certain rhythm, which in essence creates Light. When we say everything, we mean anything from a rock to a flower, a chair, a pen, an animal, water, or human. All means everything. Anything, which is everything in the universe, has a life of its own.

Now, comprehend, please, that frequency travels in streams from the Creator throughout all of time. You have heard of "A Wrinkle in Time" perhaps. Visualize this if you will, then see and imagine billions of wrinkles bending and waving like crooked lines streaming forth from a bright, golden ball, injecting the universe with life. Imagine sunbeams radiating out if this is an easier concept to grasp; millions and millions of Light beams, piercing through time from the very beginning throughout all of eternity.

You are one of the wrinkles. You are one of the sunbeams. You are never ending. You sprout from your Creator. You, in essence are the Creator because you come forth from the Creator, made in His image. We certainly must pause here and alert you to the fact that the Creative Force is neither male nor female. We now must take a moment and apologize to the ladies, but we feel most comfortable referring to the Creator as male, only because most humans feel comfortable with divine male entities. On the physical plane, male and female are only different expressions of the same component.

Now, think for a moment and consider what we have just said. Are we telling you that you are God? You may interpret this to be so. It is vital that what we tell you must be filtered through your higher consciousness so that you obtain the true essence of the truth. It could be dangerous for some of you at your present level to believe that you are God. You must visualize and see in your mind how this actually works, otherwise, it may not go so well for you. People have been martyred and killed for less throughout your earthly history. Understand that because of who you are, it is natural that you will turn an ear toward this message and hear what we have to say. You will know in the deepest core of yourself that what we tell you is the ultimate truth. To the religious our truth will be seen as evil.

We apologize and are saddened that the human condition is such that all the great wonders of truth and existence have been cleverly hidden for so long. It is with our sincere hope that we can began to infiltrate in whatever way we can. Our message is to shed Light on the truth. It is one of hope and purpose. It is for the multitudes that have cowered throughout human history in complete ignorance and fear of their once great and glorious beginnings.

Chapter Four

Accessing the Divine

What we come to tell you is not simple. There are many levels to the learning. At first as you read our message you many hear one thing, then as you read again you may hear another thing. It will not hurt to read our message over and over. What we say to you is designed so that you will absorb something different every time and each time on another level. What we tell you is highly complex. Although we have tried to prepare you to receive the information, it may still be difficult for some of you. This is your purpose though, and you know it in the very deepest part of yourself.

Know that you are designed with an ultimate purpose. You were designed as such from the very beginning. You *are* different and you know it. All your life you may feel as if you have floundered socially. This is because of your different design. Your frequency pulsates at a different rate and can cause disharmony in the presence of others. Perhaps when you were younger, this somewhat annoying problem bothered you, so much so that you had a tough time getting going in this world.

As you have grown older you have grown wiser, but not necessarily with the wisdom of the average human intelligence. Your intelligence is not human as you think of human. There *are* many different species in the Creator's Creation. When the Creator created, He went forth from Himself and worked in many varied mediums, such as an artist might do. An artist would perhaps use clay, pencil, paint or fabric. If the artist created a painting, it would be an entirely different creation than the lump of clay that has been used to mold a sculpture. So it is with the great Creator. The Creator's creations are many and varied, and they spread across the universe.

The Creator's Creations have different and various functions. Because of this, the essence of each special creation is different. Even on planet Earth, what you perceive as humankind is in actuality many species that have gathered themselves in the so-called guise of human bodies. Even so, as there may seem to be a great variety of humans scattered across the Earth, there are still so many *more* kinds of creations, some that you are totally unaware of. You are but one kind, and once again, it is here that we must stress to you the importance of your species. Now that you dwell upon Earth in human form, the body that surrounds and protects you is vital to your well being. We tell you that this human shell that protects the precious cargo inside is *very* important. Do not take it lightly and abuse it. The two have become one now that you inhabit this space called Earth. One works with the other. One is seen and one is unseen.

What is unseen is not always obvious on the surface. Often it is invisible. Others will not even realize what you are all about, although they may certainly *feel* something, but they are never quite sure what it is. You can cause discomfort just by your mere presence. On the other hand, you attract like a magnet those that are drawn to you for their own particular reasons. You may have noticed this by now, especially as you have grown older and tried to analyze human behavior along the way.

What we tell you is the truth. *You* are like a laser light shot through all of time. *You* are far more powerful than you can ever imagine. You once knew your true origin and purpose, but when you chose to come into this realm of existence on Earth, you became bogged down in heavy, powerful layers of energy that made you forget. This energy is transmitted as a kind of frequency that captures the planet and anything that exists upon it. This is a frequency generated by other creations of which you know nothing about as of now. It is also created by all creations, including humans, many of which operate negatively.

You are frequency operating within frequency. This is not always easy for you. It could be likened to trying to wade through mud. Although this would be a difficult task indeed, if you work hard enough you can accomplish the impossible. You can perform amazing feats if you only begin to realize that you were designed perfectly in order to plow your way through the thickest of mud, in other words, through the most difficult obstacles. Know that the choice is always yours. You will never be forced, but please, believe us when we tell you that you *do* have a divine purpose and if you neglect to do your job, you *will* feel the results. Some great God is certainly not punishing you, but to ignore that which you were designed for will cause you to suffer somewhat from the consequences.

What we tell you cannot be taken lightly. You must always listen and read carefully. Read again and again the same paragraph if you must, but please make absolutely sure that you absorb to the best of your ability the spiritual knowledge that we impart to you.

We are here to inform you. We *will* unlock the secrets and you *will* begin to unfold like an accordion. Layer by layer, you *will* begin to remember. You may experience irritability, frustration, lethargy and even depression as you go through these changes. Please, do not be dismayed. These are only temporary symptoms of your rapid evolvement and will improve dramatically. We regret the inconvenience this fine-tuning of your frequency will bring to you in your present life. Understand that this adjustment will not only benefit you here at this point in time, but will also travel backwards and forward to effect *all* that you are.

It is important that you realize the scope of your mission and to accomplish what many believe is impossible. There will often be times when you, yourself, will believe that it is impossible. So, it is beforehand that we want to warn you. This is one of *our* tasks, to warn you and to help you. Believe us when we tell you there are many on Earth at this time that *want* to see you fail. Sometimes if you dare to say the slightest thing that seems out of the norm, you will be laughed at and ridiculed, even by the very people that claim to be your friends. Do not be deceived, but continue and pursue that which you must.

Search for the answers within and you will know what to do. We, also, will always be there, helping and guiding and leading the way. Be sensitive to that which is in your heart. Trust your feelings and follow them, for where you find feeling, you will always find your higher self. If you are reading this, it may be that your higher self is Pleiadian! We operate on the love frequency, so it is vital that you make every attempt to stay away from that which *feels* bad. You will know when it is not right. You will have a certain feeling, and although you cannot avoid everything bad, it is not in your best interest to stick around when things are negative.

You will not necessarily need to change others by your outward actions. In fact, open displays of anger and hostility will only lead you down other paths that will cause you to deviate from your truest purpose. Many tricks are designed that will cause you to intentionally stumble. You will fall prey to these clever tactics if you do not stay alert.

There will be many times in your life where it will seem that other people instigate your problems and worries. You will of course want to react and pursue and get lost in these many dramas that you often call *life*. You must discipline yourself to stay afloat, and to often rise above the circumstances and even the people. It is only by doing this that you will learn to navigate within *all* situations and circumstances.

Please, do not be dismayed. It is not as difficult as all that. You were designed for this purpose, and you, my friend, are connected to a Light source that others often stray away from. All you must do is pull this Light into yourself to activate *all* that you are. Rise above any and all conditions and situations. Imagine in your mind that you are gliding up, up, up, riding a beam of Light. You are calm, composed and serene as the Light pulls you upward.

Believe and know in your heart that you never, never *have* to participate in those things which are not of your choosing. All that is necessary is to pull away and imagine yourself hovering in the Light over or away from the situation. It will protect you. It will keep you.

We will tell you many of the same things over and over in many different ways and forms, although you will not always realize this is being done. There is always a plan to our every word, thought and action. Please know this, and that the content of this message has not been brought to you in a haphazard way. There are levels upon levels, going from easy to difficult, from complex to highly complex. It is necessary to speak to you on one level, then proceed to another level and another and another, all in the same information source. What you are reading now contains multiple layers of the same information. You will input what you can handle on one level, and as you access information, you will actually accelerate to the point in your development where you will be able to receive more and more on a higher level. After awhile, you will arrive at a place where it will no longer be necessary to gather information from physical sources. You, yourself, will become

Accessing the Divine

a receiver of all that is divine. As you think, so shall you receive, your brain acting as a computer to store, distribute and encode information.

You are under the impression that computers are powerful tools of communication. Many of you are consumed for hours at your computers, totally engrossed in accessing information and storing it. You give up your perceived physical reality, even giving up real people in order to connect with strangers all over the world. How is it that you know to whom you speak? Yet, you do it so casually, as if perusing the world in this manner was just an ordinary every day event. My friend, what you have is great faith. You know that you know when you push the button on your computer that some kind of activity will take place. You never doubt it, right? In fact, you expect it. You will connect with others, even bond with perfectly anonymous strangers, and it will seem normal to you. You will even gather tremendous amounts of information, storing it all in your files. It is so amazing and *so* easy to do. .

May we suggest something here? Push another button if you will. Right now, imagine that you have pushed a hidden button to an unseen world. Go ahead, try it. Did many icons appear? Probably not. Do you know why? It is because you are conditioned to believe in what you think you can see with your eyes. When you were a baby, even a small child, perhaps even an older child, you saw

43

things that you could not possibly see now. Perhaps you remember some of those things. In fact, you think and wonder about those "odd" little things often. You can never really locate or place them neatly into your compact view of reality.

Imagine pushing the button again. Actually, physically poke the air now with your finger. There *is* a button there, and it *will* open other worlds, but you must have the same amount of faith that you have when your turn on your computer. You know when you push the button on the computer that it will come on and open whole new worlds for you to view, experience and participate in.

So it is with your invisible button. Push it often and expect to see things that you cannot ordinarily see with your physical eyes.

Chapter Five

Possessing the
Knowledge of Light

Our chapters will not be overly long. We want to speak to you in short powerful bursts. We do not want to detain you for too long at any one particular time; especially when there is so much to do in your reality. We do hope to have your full attention as you are reading this. If you need to go, but are rushing to finish a long chapter, perhaps you will miss something that is vital.

What you perceive to be physical in your world is hardly physical at all. It would even be possible for you to stick your finger through anything you wanted. All that is, and all that you see, is only a manifestation of what you think you should see. Your illusions are solidly planted. In a way, they manifest in a physical sense because that is what is necessary to maintain your reality.

Frequency vibrates and forms to create what appear as solid objects. Even human bodies appear as solid. Please know that everything in all realities are composed of the same kind of frequency. The frequency emanates from the Great Creator and is part of this source. Anything manifested as reality as you know it has its source in the Creator. Frequency is the Creator. All that you observe, all that you know and understand originates there. Now, think of the Creator as a huge energy source, as beams that burst forth and shoot throughout all of time. The beams are crackling with energy and this creates the vibration. All up and down the millions of vibrational beams, realities of physical manifestations pop into existence. What you are now is but one point in the vast array of creation.

Frequencies have the capacity to move things, although this is a simple way of stating it. Frequency, if intensified enough, creates something solid. In other words, we might say that solidity is based on frequencies. If all solid things are in actuality, only frequency, then you might begin to see how easily things are movable or penetrable. This is the secret to many of the unexplainable mysteries of the ancient world. Beings that existed then knew how to use and navigate through frequencies. They knew how to transport what you, in this time sequence, see as the impossible. They understood how to move a huge block from here to there without any effort at all. In fact, many of the great pyramids were built in this manner simply by manipulating frequencies. If you could observe this in your day and age you would probably say it was mind over matter.

Watching things move and change, while one concentrates, certainly can appear to be one thing on one level, but is an entirely different thing on another level. We want to tell you that it is all a matter of frequency and not anything really mystical at all. If the rock seems solid in one place, then all you have to do is bend the frequency in another place and the rock appears there. This is not always a simple concept to grasp in your reality at the present time, but it is something that you must begin to think about and begin to explore.

Understand that this kind of knowledge could be dangerous in the wrong hands. We realize this, but we present it to you nevertheless, knowing that it is something that most people would never pursue with any seriousness. But, you are different. By offering you this knowledge, you will file it into your memory banks and you will begin to remember. As you remember, you will think about it and you will eventually grow into all that you are.

All that you are contains more than you realize. Because you are frequency trapped within frequency, we come and bring you the message that you long ago pre-arranged with us to do. We are friends and have a close and personal relationship. Our friendship is closer than close for we are one and the same and we work toward a common goal. We are an extension of you going forward and you are an extension of us going backward. Because we help you, you help us. You knew, as we knew from the beginning, that this would be the way we would work together.

Many of you do not remember and a book may be necessary to jog your memories. As you read and absorb, you will begin to expand and remember. It is even possible that perhaps you have heard or read these messages before. Yes, we have come to you many times during your present life cycle, yet it will take many more awakenings for you to remember and begin to act. There are many of you in the Light Family, but not all of you will be activated in this present cycle. Some of our family members are here to experience growth, then they will move on to other places and help there.

Each of you will be used in different ways and for purposes that will complete the goal. Each of you are talented in different areas, but nevertheless, your intention is to further the creation by what you bring in. Understand though, that what you possess is the knowledge of Light, and by possessing this knowledge, you are capable of passing and leaving information.

Some of you will be receptors for information, such as that which you are reading now. You will absorb and pass along what you learn. Others will automatically know and verbalize what they have learned from Divine Oneness. Others, by their mere actions, will show or display information that is needed by all for the continual evolution of creation. We might tell you that the process of getting the information across or spreading the Light, if you will, is going to be distributed in varying amounts to each of you. It will be as if you each are gifted in different areas. If you know that you are Light, and you are reading a book such as this one, you will be absorbing vital information into yourself, thus, you will grow and evolve at a tremendous rate. As you gain knowledge, you in return will spread knowledge in some way, fashion or form. You can trust us on this matter.

Now, speaking of another sort of matter, matter is energy and energy is always movable. Frequencies create energy and it becomes solid matter. Everything in your existence has been materialized from frequencies and appears as matter. Believe us when we tell you that everything you see is only an illusion. Illusions are capable of vanishing. Have you ever lost something such a needle or a pen when it was just there a moment ago?

All matter requires tremendous energy to keep it focused as something solid and material. You do not realize at this time just how much all of you energize frequencies to create what you believe is a solid world made of matter. Yes, collective consciousness forms and pools together without you ever being aware that it is going on. It is as if this huge whirling pool of specialized energy keeps everything afloat. When individual consciousness refuses to conform to the mass collective consciousness, problems and conflicts arise on Earth. If individual thought forms do not merge completely, then matter itself can be shaken, or even destroyed, or can simply vanish!

These are processes that you are completely unaware of, but they can be compared to breathing or the beating of the heart. Most of you cannot or would not attempt to control your breathing or your heart rate. Such as you cannot control these natural functions of the human body, neither can you control the realm where matter is created. We are only here to inform you of these things, to bring you information so as to start the eventual process of higher evolution.

Our job is to make you think, to help change you, and to cause you to act or react. We want you to realize the power that lies within you. The power is yours to control and do that which you will to a certain extent, although there will always be limitations because of the frequency at which you vibrate. This power in most of you at this time is minuscule, so do not be discouraged or dismayed. The power will increase as your knowledge increases.

You are different because you sprout from a Light source. We do not want you to be deceived. Not all creation comes directly from Light. As there is Light, so is there Darkness. Darkness abounds in all corners of the universe and throughout all of creation itself. Be forewarned, darkness is an enemy of Light in the sense that it is contrary and opposite to Light. Do not be dismayed by this knowledge. The darkness always sounds foreboding, but the real power is always in the Light. You are capable of shining with such brilliance that you can blast through Darkness with ease. You must believe this and always know it to be true. Light is always greater than Darkness, although Darkness can certainly be oppressive. It can feel very bad, but only if you allow yourself to be pulled into its murky depths.

Does not the Sun shine with more brilliance than the moon? Think on this for only a moment and then you will begin to see. The moon is indeed beautiful in all its many forms, and you may gaze at it intently, but it is the Sun which lights the world. The Sun makes life, as you know it, although you take it for granted and never really think about it. You completely forget that this ball of Light is that which lights your way. So it is with those that emanate with Light and those that emanate with Darkness.

It is here that we pause, having to inform you of your true origin. You come from Light, and that is why you are Light. The essence of all that you are was created in Light. Do not be surprised when we tell you that you originated from the Sun, yet the Sun is not what you really think it to be. The Sun is emanating at a certain frequency to maintain the illusion of what it appears to be in your world. To you, it is a big ball of fire and gases and nothing more. This is the nature of the Sun in your reality, just as the nature of all that you are in this reality is certainly different than what you think it to be.

You are frequency, but your frequency is different in that your origin began with the Sun. The Sun, also, is frequency, but another kind of frequency. If you can think of all that you might imagine God to be, then think of the Sun in the same manner.

To some of you this might be a totally bizarre concept to believe that your very familiar Sun is any kind of God. You might think this is more than blasphemous or just plain silliness, but please know, here and now, that all things are not always what they seem to be. You hold your illusions well, including your concept of the Sun. In actuality, not only the sun, but all Light bodies in the sky are recorded simply as Light in this reality. Here, their purpose is to light the sky, whether it be by night or by day. In another reality, all Light bodies in the sky are something entirely different than what you perceive them to be.

Chapter Six

Connecting On Deeper Levels

Throughout your human history as you know it, people have always connected themselves in relationship to the heavenly bodies. This knowledge has been passed down through the generations. In the deepest part of you, the part that streams throughout all of time, the correlation between your body and the heavenly Light bodies is very well known. On Earth, what you know as astrology is but a small, minute particle of all that really is. You are connected on a much deeper level than most of you could ever suspect.

Your very origin is wrapped up with what you perceive to be Light bodies in the sky. In the *Light Family*, your origins are in the sun. There are many suns that you call stars, but *all* are one and the same and are interconnected. You perceive that which you believe to be a sky full of twinkling lights as separate bodies. It is now that we tell you this is a wrong perception. They are not separate at all, although in your reality you perceive the night sky as it appears to be scattered with pinpoints of Light. Believe us, things are not always as they appear.

Please know that all suns are connected and operate as one unit in another reality. Think of the majesty, the beauty and glory of God if you could amass every sun in every universe and fit them together as one radiant, magnificent, shimmering light mass. This is creation from the beginning. This is Power and Energy. This is Light Divine. This is the origin of your creation. You, who are Light, have been thrown off as an extension of your Creator. *You* are from the Light. You *are* Light, and it may be that you are different from others.

Who are these others? We must tell you there are quite an assortment on planet Earth. You may have suspected that by now as you have traveled along your path encountering many, many different people along the way. Think about it, is this not true? Think again about all the people that have come and gone in your life. So many perhaps, but so few that you have truly and genuinely connected with. In fact, you have felt the opposition from many, no doubt. You, as humans, do not always realize that you navigate not only through words and physical gestures, but in the spiritual realm as well. In fact, it is true that most of your interaction takes place in an unseen spiritual realm that you may not even consciously recognize. It is on this level that you know more about each other than you perceive on a conscious level. You know also, that when you encounter Darkness you are automatically repulsed. Often, and even in most cases, you do not make the connection, but spiritually you know to stay away.

There are many, many life forms on Earth that originate from other places and not the Sun. The Sun, connected as one to other suns is the Ultimate of Creators. It is Light and it creates *only* Light.

Every cell of your being is a receptor. You attract Light to your cells. If you know nothing else, please know this, for Light is power. You must make every effort to never forget that it is Light that conquers and controls you. We do not speak of conquer and control in negative terms, but in a higher sense in that Light is your determining factor. It is Light that guides you and leads you and shows you the way. Light permeates all and even shines through the Darkness, and it is on this frequency that you ride. The Darkness lurks in every corner. Because you are Light, you have the ability to pierce the Dark with the Light that you possess. It is good for you to begin to learn and understand your own power.

In so many of your movies, TV shows and even children's programming, the prevalent theme is usually one of Light versus Dark, or good versus evil. This is a common thread that weaves itself through much of your so-called entertainment industry. Think about it. Why does this happen? It happens because each and every one of you understands subconsciously that some of you possess goodness and others possess evil. The question we present, and it might be a thought provoking one at that, is why do you choose to deal with good and evil issues as entertainment?

We must point out to you that it is not entertainment in the actual sense that you are being entertained, but instead, much of what you like to *call* entertainment is a glimpse into other realities. For many of you, this is the only way to gather this knowledge so that you can consciously recognize it as part of your fabric. As you absorb that which is presented to you, you grasp at a deeper level what it is all about. Some people do not need to view this reality as presented in a movie or TV shows, because certain parts of their knowledge have already been completed. This knowledge of which we speak is not anything so blatant that you instantly recognize it, but it is information received at a much deeper and subtle level. Sometimes watching movies and TV is good and other times it is not. Sometimes there can be an input of information that seems to destroy or damage, although the inner being can always sort it out and categorize, such as it will, according to the individual rate of development.

"Know that all things work together for good." This is a quote from the Bible and we like it so much we would like to use it here. It is good and advantageous to memorize this particular quote for it will do much to help you through this existence. The *good* is the *ultimate good,* although it may not always be recognized in one single reality. As your consciousness streams throughout time, the goodness of creation will result because each and every one of you will have experienced *all.* As it is now, you are learning to be whole and full, not only here, but in many, many other dimensions.

Sometimes life as you know it can seem bleak, and you might certainly begin to question the sanity of it all. Know that *all* things do indeed work together for good, and this will see you through many adventures, both good and bad.

Sometimes there will seem to be more bad in life than there is good. Perhaps it is here that we should tell you that in your present Earth reality, there are more bad entities than there are good, thus making Earth's energy heavy with Darkness. It is through this Darkness that you must wade. As we have said before, you have the ability to pierce the Darkness with a *Sword of Light,* but let us warn you in advance that you will not always be appreciated.

You will feel alone much of the time, as you seem to battle unseen forces and physical obstacles on Earth. Although we can tell you that it will not always be easy, know in your heart that you are *not* alone. We are here to tell you that you have a multitude of *good* forces on your side. Although they may remain invisible to you, they surround you and invade your space with frequency of the highest order. You are the Light and you come equipped for battle. All you have to do is trust your inner voice. Follow it where you will, for when you follow, there you will find the truth of yourself. In finding this inner truth, you will be able to navigate successfully into life's many battles.

Your job is twofold. Since you are an extension of Light, coming from the Creator at the beginning, you shine like a beacon throughout all of time. You will open up portals of energies that are closed or have been closed. Once these portals are open, the Darkness will not be allowed to enter, for this domain is totally yours and gateways will be created that lead to other dimensions. Nothing harmful will be allowed into these other places, only more and more Light will come until it spreads like a shimmering cover over all.

What you perceive in the night skies is nothing compared to that which is coming. You gaze on a clear night and perhaps try to experience the emotional intensity of the universe. It is incomprehensible, is it not? Where does it begin, where does it end? Your mind cannot grasp the concept of infinity. All you can see with your physical eyes is that which you see spread out above you. Then it appears to simply end, although you know that it does not, but you are incapable of seeing that which you do not know. You may struggle with the thought of infinity as your mind attempts to grasp and hold onto this concept.

Your problem is knowing that you cannot see that which you know to be. What you perceive above is dependent on the reality that your frequency is tuned to. At the present time, the reality that you exist at is a low frequency one. Low frequency realities permit more of the physical aspects. Higher frequency realities vibrate to a faster pitch thus enabling the physical to fade away as the energy of the Light source permeates more.

Although we operate in your very distant future, we are not permeated with pure Light energy as of yet. There are beings that are far more evolved than we are, and yes, we *all* work together to effect the ultimate outcome of all creation. We do realize, however, that in your particular dimension of time, things are not going so well. Although we are from your future, we ride the same exact frequency wave that you do. If this is not obviously clear, imagine Light beams streaming from the Sun. Imagine also, if you will, other energies created from other cosmic sources. Although all of creation is ultimately connected, it is you and it is us that are one and the same, operating harmoniously as one unit. In a sense we are the same sunbeam, and we will keep shining and shining forever and will never stop. Now, visualize this sunbeam with many, many stops along its way. It is at these stops that we get off and on, experiencing the dimensional realities that we call *life*. When we speak of life, we do not always mean the life that you are experiencing now. The many varieties of so called life are as varied as the grains of sand on a beach, but you *will* experience them all.

Reincarnation is a simplified term of *all* that is. Yes, it is true that you have many lives, but they do not come in succession, one right after another. Life is not linear, but is built layer upon layer, projecting forward and backward. It expands outward in ever widening circles like a stone dropped in water, only in this case the ripple never ends. You might say that life is indeed multi-layered. It is so complex that the human mind has difficulty grasping it, although we must say that throughout all of history many attempts have been made. So it is that throughout human evolution there have always been people to convey spiritual knowledge and wisdom. In many cases these special people have often been one of your fellow Light Family Members. Know that not all information has been the same, but it is the wisdom contained therein that helps to further the spiritual advancement and development of creation.

There are many spiritual levels operating at once within Earth's frequency. This is why there so often seems to be confusion. Know that it is important for you to understand that there will be different levels of spiritual development. This is true because of the abundance of many varieties of creations operating within one frequency. Even within what appears to be the human species, know that there are multitudes of different species, yet all are contained in the same package....the human body.

We suggest you have a closer look. Have you ever found one human that looks like another? This is no accident, but *all* have been designed by a great and wonderful plan. The spiritual came first, seemingly invisible in all but the highest level of frequencies. Every one of us were made first in the spiritual realm, and express our creativity by our variety of physical forms in the lower frequency realities. In the higher realms, spiritual variety is expressed in different ways and not always as solidly as it is in the lower realms. It is more of an expression of Light. You might even say that *all* glows within these higher realms and could even be perceived as heavenly!

Knowing the Mind of God

There have been those throughout human history that have glimpsed other worlds. It is not only possible for the mystics to see into these worlds, but it is possible for *you* also. You have the capacity not only to see, but also to enter into other realities. You do this all the time, although you are not always fully conscious of it.

Life is extremely complex, far more complex than you might understand, so it is with much anticipation that we hope you find in-Lightenment here. We would like to jog your memory cells to help you to fully awaken, for in your very deepest self you know there is so much more. It is with much regret that we must tell you how our hearts have been deeply saddened, as we have continually and repeatedly confronted you throughout your lifetime. You have not always heard, or you have heard and have not responded. You have even chosen to ignore the voice within, even when you came close and started to listen. Although we have been saddened, we have never given up the pursuit, even though it has required much effort and determination on our part.

We come to you now in the form of words, although you have seen us in your dreams and possibly even experienced us as in your physical reality. Do not be surprised at this statement, as we have told you that life is complex. Creation is not as simple as you may think. It is even possible that we have been intertwined with you for a lifetime. At this point you may be racking your memory trying to remember when you last felt any sort of presence or being by your side. Please, do not suddenly be overcome with fear and leave us again. Our intention is not to frighten you, but to in-Lighten you. Any fear that you may experience is generated by you, and you alone. You fear that which you do not understand. We come to bring you understanding. We come in whatever way is best for you. Know that being intertwined with you does not always mean a physical pursuit, but it may be that we operate within the layers of your sub-conscious mind.

We bring you information, and please believe us when we tell you that this information is vital to *all* of Creation. You have a job to do. It is probably by far the most important job on Earth. You must be worthy of it. To achieve worthiness, you must absorb and believe with all your heart what you know to be truth. Go within yourself. It is possible that you will find this truth. If you do not find it here, then it will certainly not be *your* truth and you will have to move on.

If you stay with us, we are happy to reveal information concerning your existence. *You* are Light. Know that Light sheds truth on Darkness. Think of the night and all that goes on under the cover of blackness. There is much hidden, is there not? Think of what would happen if someone pierced the Darkness with a beam of Light? *You*, my friend are that Beam of Light. *You*, and others like you will shed truth on Darkness. All you have to do is listen. Listen to that which you might perceive as God speaking to you in your heart. With a rational mind, confirm what you know by how you feel. Does it feel right?

We would like to tell you that, *yes*, God still does speak to people in their hearts and not only through books. There are many that quote scripture upon scripture from the Bible, or from other Holy books, believing they are speaking God's mind. Yes, they may be doing just that, but others are also. Know that God, the Ultimate Spirit and your Creator, created you, and still lives and speaks as one spirit through you.

By closing off your mind to the voice of God, you shut out much information that is vital to your evolvement. Again, we must warn you at this point that all the voices you may hear within you, and even outside of yourself are not the voice of your Ultimate Creator. There are many voices. You may ask, how is it that you will know the *true* one? As Children of Light, you will *always* know the truth. It is those creations which are not of the Light that will have difficulty. They will make mistakes and they will flounder. They will search for answers within and without, but will never really find that which they seek in this lifetime.

As we have told you, there are many species of life now flourishing upon your Earth. Not all are created in the Light. You may have gone for a very long time being tricked and fooled, but we tell you again, not all are created in the Light. There are many more created from Darkness, but who search for their own truth. Do not be too concerned with their search. We do not mean to sound cold hearted, but these *others* will simply never know what you know, nor understand all that is. Their ultimate destiny takes them down another path entirely and is a separate one than yours.

You may be tricked many times, thinking the deeply religious are good and are created in the Light. They may attend church, read their Bibles, and basically appear to be good and moral, but be not fooled my friend, for they can indeed be wolves in sheep's clothing. It may be as difficult for you to know their true intention as it is difficult for them to know yours, for they may genuinely believe that you are the enemy. Because of this, you may encounter many frustrating moments as you tread upon the Earth trying to find those to which you connect and belong.

You will know those of the darkness when they try to prevent you from acquiring more information. They will stifle your curiosity and call your dreams wicked and evil. They will want to put blinders on you to prevent you from knowing the truth. They want to see you confined and shut up in a small, dark box, too afraid to venture forth as you reach for answers that belong to you.

We are saddened that we must shatter your illusions, but expand your mind enough to see that often what you call your Holy books are simply cleverly designed devices to keep you blind and in the dark. Your Holy books dictate laws that purposely shut off all further exploration to find out what and who you really are. Of course, there is always the *good*, but as we have said before, it is often cleverly designed so that the truth has been mixed with much that is not the truth. Please know that there have been many so called Holy men and women that are deceived themselves, because that which is good does not always control them.

We want to tell you it is always to your benefit to find out what you can. In the Light, all is exposed and you will find that there is both good and evil. You are Light and therefore you will be capable of taking the truth into yourself. This will burst the doors of your soul wide open. You will begin to see that much of what humans believe to be true is in fact many tales and even lies woven into intricate stories. These lies have been perpetrated to draw in those of the Light, and thus to squelch information, knowledge of truth and the true meaning of creation. To know the true meaning is to know the freedom of expression.

Sadly to say, there are those that would like to see all of creation scattered and upset. We think of them as troublemakers of the worst sort, but we have to tell you that they are indeed powerful and their effects trickle throughout all time levels. These beings have their own agenda, but then, so do you. Be aware of them, but do not be so consumed with their negative forces that you cannot do your job.

As we are able to pop into your time frequency, there are also others that can do the same. We may appear to some of you in a physical form, but our intention is never to frighten you. We regret that many of you have observed and even been involved with many species of less desirable origins that come to you from other dimensions. You often cannot consciously pick us out from those that have less honorable intentions. Know that you are us and we are you and our Creator is one and the same and protects us both. You are Light and you are far more powerful than you may realize. It is our ultimate destiny that Light will conquer and rule, for our God is the Ultimate Creator of *all.* In the end, *all* will go back to God. For now, this is a paradox that we will explain later and in more detail.

What you should know at this point is that many of the Lesser Gods are troubled. Yes, we call them gods, and their images have been fashioned from many substances and their shapes and forms exist all over the world. You may see them even in children's cartoons and toys. In many countries around the world, ancient people worshipped these gods. Even today they continue to make their likenesses. As these ugly reptilian and birdlike creatures represent the lesser evil gods, please know they are ultimately *not* the Supreme God at all, but they did and still do give birth to their own creations.

Yes, so it is true that many of what you perceive as humans are in actuality creations of the Lesser Gods. As all time exists at once, they too are spread into eternity from the beginning to the end. We have told you that you are like a sunbeam, and yes, all vibrates as frequency, but not all are likened to sunbeams. If frequency could be perceived in a sort of Light spectrum, yours would glow like a bright Light, while others of the Lesser Gods would be dull and dark, hardly emitting anything but a faint hint of gray.

That is why you will be recognized by many, not only in this dimension, but in others as well. You may even find yourself being tormented, but because you vibrate with Light, you can overcome. It is not always necessary to verbalize what you know and feel or to fight and struggle, for that only fuels the darkness and robs you of your power as you flee in hopelessness and frustration.

We want to help by giving you this important information. Know that it is vital for you to understand that arguing and fighting is not the answer for you. The emotion you feel at such times is turbulant and unsettling. It is only a physical manifestation of what lies inside of you. In other words, what you reflect outwardly is what you contain inwardly. Extreme and detrimental emotion only feeds the lower elements of your nature and can cause you much trouble as you navigate your realm. It is possible that others want to upset and antagonize you, even if consciously they are unaware of their intentions and motives. On another level, they know that you are Light. If they can upset you, your frequency will waver and affect things that you are not aware of yet.

We give you the key, which is to do your best to maintain your composure at all times. This composure we speak of is spiritual in nature. You must go within your own spirit, take a deep breath and draw Universal Light unto yourself. Trust that the Light will fill you completely, for you are composed of this Light. It will keep you and protect you. This is spiritual composure. You will need it for anything having to do with matters in your world and even not of your world. What we are talking about is spirit fighting spirit, as spirit is indeed contained in all things. This is not something that you are necessarily aware of. If you find yourself withering inside and even floundering because of spiritual attacks, know that this is spirit fighting with spirit. Pull in the Light, please, and know who you are.

Some of you that are Light creations are finding that perhaps your marriages are suffering and you have become disheartened. You are no doubt beginning to question how you ended up in this predicament. It seemed so right in the beginning. There are no accidents, our dear friend, and what was to be is exactly what is. There is a purpose to *all* unions, whether it is Light with Light or Light with Darkness. There are many answers, and we might only suggest a few, but our hope is that you are helped. Light chooses Darkness in order to teach and in-Lighten, the only problem being that in human form, Light does not always recognize Darkness. What you thought you could in-Lighten, you now find, after perhaps many years, will never be in-Lightened. Our only suggestion for this dilemma is that you never, never have to stay and try to function as one in spirit. You will never be one spirit with Darkness.

Sometimes Darkness chooses Light in order to diminish the Light. If enough Darkness can overcome and influence the Light, the ultimate effects of the outcome of all creation will be diminished. Of course, this may be the intention of the lesser forces, but the power of Light has been underestimated. All malevolent purposes and designs will be revealed. The time has come, dear friend. It is up to you, and to all those created of the Light, to receive this and any other vital information and to pass it among yourselves.

Because you are Light existing in this time frequency, most of you will ultimately find the correct information that will be right for you. It will empower and enable you to continue that which you were created for. You were created by a Great and Divine Spirit to experience life and to experience it abundantly. Much of the woes and miseries in your lives has been caused by the interference of the Lesser Gods. Know that this was part of the plan and there are no mistakes. Know also, that the original creations of Light will burst onto the scene and change the course of creation, thus enabling all to ultimately translate into Light.

As we have told you, God is not actually a male entity, but a living, vibrating essence of *all that is.*

God is like a powerful, pulsating, breathing entity of which there is no other. We *all* emanate from this source, which not only extends into all of time, but also extends into universe after universe after universe. God's creations are so numerous that it would boggle the mind to experience and see them all. In fact, the human mind is so small that it could not comprehend *all* that God is or what this name implies.

You may wonder if we ourselves comprehend the magnitude of what it is that we are telling you. We must say that since we are your future selves and exist far into another realm, we comprehend a bit more than you do, but still, our comprehension is not complete. As we project into the distant future and communicate with Light beings that you do not yet know, we see that there is so much to learn, yet so much that you can do to help now. Helping yourselves and others to awaken will ultimately help and serve all of creation.

The processes that you must go through to find answers and make discoveries will take a lifetime. Even then you will continue the process into other lives and beyond. Your soul is ever widening and never ending, spreading eternally across time. As your Light manifests in each realm, you are still part of the same Light, unfolding and evolving to all that you are.

It would please us very much if you would take into your heart what you have learned and apply it to the processes that you will encounter in your journey. As you become familiar with our teachings, you will learn to recognize us and not be afraid. Our only intent is that you feel comfortable in your mind and heart with what we bring. We honor you always, thus our highest purpose is to help you in whatever ways that we possibly can.

Jumping Dimensions

It is possible to literally transcend your human body. Although all humans do this naturally when sleeping, most have no idea that they can do it while awake. In fact, most have no idea they can even come out of their bodies. The body and the spirit are two different things entirely, but are fused together and exist as one at the human level. Know that there are levels where the spirit is indeed hampered by having a body.

We ourselves are capable of choosing whatever we want. This perhaps might be a difficult concept to grasp, but know that we are your future and this means that one day you too will be able to choose your outer covering at will just as we do. We exist as a type of spirit in our world, but even at this level we often prefer to shroud ourselves in something more solid. Think of it as dressing in clothes perhaps.

If we come into your world, we can be as spirit or we can appear as human, or even as animals and plants. You have not arrived at this level yet. There *have* been those that have been able to enter into animals or even other humans. Although it is impossible to take on and form your own shape at this point, it *is* possible to get out of your body. Actually, it is quite easy, but many of you do not realize it. Slipping out of your body enables you to travel not only in your world, but also into different time sequences. What you appear to be in this reality is not what you always appear to be in another reality.

You may be a little confused at this point, as we have told you that all of time exists at the same time. Perhaps you would like to ask us how is it that you jump from one dimension to another and from body to body. We tell you that it really only appears that way. You exist in each reality stretching through time. It may only seem that you get out of your body as you experience another dimension. This may seem like a contradiction, but only because you are trying to grasp what we tell you. As you visualize it in your mind, the picture may grow fuzzy as you struggle to comprehend. Not only is the Earth gridlocked in negative energy, but the human mind is locked up as well. This energy is generated by sources outside of yourself. It circulates around you like a foggy mist, in a way, trapping you so that you are unable to see that which you know to be the truth.

At this point, do not be too concerned with trying to comprehend all that we tell you. We will have much opportunity to guide you into all understanding. We are beginning slowly here, and will work with you until complete comprehension comes. Let us assure you that as you process the information that we give you, your frequency will be raised to a higher level and you will vibrate to a greater tune. Yes, tune, you heard us correctly. Cosmic vibrations do create a sort of harmonious overall tune throughout creation.

All of the world's music is crude and unappealing when compared to the music of the Cosmos. The music created and generated by humans is only a very pale imitation of something you know within your deepest selves. Even the finest of earthly music is a mere attempt at duplicating the Divine music that you know intuitively. If you were able to hear the vibrational tunes that all frequencies create, you would probably be overcome with such joy and emotion that you would not be able to contain it. In the meantime, until you return to that which you came, musicians will continue to make music. People will continue to listen, all attempting to hear and know the Divine perfection of harmony once again.

Humans often become confused when it comes to music. There are many that are inspired by the Earthly condition to create melodies that only serve to excite the body and the physical senses. Although some music has been inspired by a glimpse into the Cosmos, most music is solidly rooted to Earth, having no similarity to the music of the Divine. Much of Earth's music has been created in the lower realms, although beautiful music has also been created and has its parallels in the higher more developed realms. There is also Light inspired music that has been directly influenced by the Earthly experience and comes in all shape and forms.

Our hope is to in-Lighten you in all areas. By elevating your consciousness, we are helping to increase your frequency. You will shine brighter, thus affecting the earth experience of all. As you grow in knowledge and as the Light goes from dim to bright within you, you will definitely have an impact on the reality in which you exist. You will also impact other realities with the Light of your soul. Know that you are constantly jumping dimensions. Your soul does not remain stagnant in one place but travels in and out of the many realms of reality. What you perceive in a dream is another realm in which you go.

Our intention is to bring you knowledge of the highest order. Our goal is to bring you Hope and

Light so that you will begin to affect your world. Understand that all that you do will influence the past, present and future, as well as the ultimate outcome of all that exists.

Without Hope, all is lost. Without Light, all is uninspired and dead. It is our Hope that as many, many Lights are lit all over the world, things will begin to brighten. The frequency grids will crackle with energy so strong and powerful that the Light generated will begin to seep into the darkest corners. *You* are important. *You* are vital to a very worthy cause. As you and others begin to seek and find each other, your energy levels will begin to increase as you lock together to form powerful unions.

Know there are many scattered around the Earth that we are bringing information to. What you know, they will know. What they know, you will also know. We tell you that you generate far more power as a complete and whole unit, thus it is vital that you begin to find each other. It is now, in your current time frequency that this can be easily done. Before the age of extensive electronic communication and widely circulated books in every language, this was rather an impossible task.

All over the planet there are those that weave tales of woe and stories of destruction concerning the end times. We come to tell you the truth as others have also. Understand that there are many,

many realities, and it is possible to choose that which will affect the reality you find yourself in. Some realities are not what they appear to be and are calculated in a way to lead you toward another and perhaps more destructive reality. Know that cleverly designed tactics can be put in place to lead you astray and to make you believe things that are not true.

You must arm yourself with the correct information. You will learn through experience to recognize us and others of the Light. Although there will be those that shun you, and even laugh and ridicule you, it is our hope that you will find us as your guides. We will help lead you into knowledge and truth or at least provide you with some satisfactory answers. With our diligent help, you and others of the Light will eventually be able to know creation as it should be. You will actually change the course and direction of realities as they collapse and converge as if a stack of blocks, one on top of the other.

Yes, there are many versions of the final outcome of Creation. You will begin to contain the secret because you will hear a small voice whispering in your ear. Already, this unknown secret has wafted over and around you for an entire lifetime as you have strained to hear it. Listen to it, for with the help of God, which is at the highest aspect of your soul, we also intersect to bring you information from another dimension. We will instruct you on how to focus your energy so that you will be able to shine a direct beam into the darkness. Remember, your power is because of that which you emanate from. You do not stand alone, nor are you protected when you *try* to stand alone. You are a direct beam from the Source of *all* Power. Because the Creator is Light, *you* also are Light.

Time is changing. You may have begun to sense this in recent years. Something feels different because it *is* different. Imagine numerous layers of realities stacked one on top of another like a great, huge stack of assorted pancakes. Within each pancake the substances are different, as with each reality the story is different. Someone is compressing the stack of pancakes at both ends. As they smash together their substances will soon become one with only those ingredients contained to make up one solitary pancake. So it is with all of time and with all realities. No doubt you have heard various stories concerning the end times. This is only because many different realities exist at once, but what is left in the end will be the only one as far as you are concerned.

We hope you are beginning to see how simple it would be to choose the ending. We say this with a smile, knowing we have penetrated an area in your mind and soul, thus shedding new Light in an area that was once dark. In other words, we hope you have seen the Light!

It will not be easy to recognize each other solely based on physical characteristics. This is why it grieves us to watch the turmoil on Earth between the different races. How will you ever find one another with participation in such nonsense? What you are is not dependent on skin color at all. We must stress again that this is pure nonsense at its very worst. We must warn you that as a Child of Light, you must *never, never* determine someone's spirit by their skin color. Skin color is irrelevant. As we have told you before, the Great Creator designed all using different mediums. It is that simple. The Creator used black and white, red and yellow. There is truth to the children's song that God loves *all* of His creations. So it is with Divine law. You, also, are expected to love one another no matter what the outer covering.

It may sound like a contradiction when we tell you to love all creations, when we have gone to great lengths to inform you of the darker forces. For now, that is the best policy to operate under as many are without the proper discernment to know who good and who is bad. So we say to you that it is best to love all. This does not necessarily mean that you should take everyone you meet into your home and smother them with love. Just tread carefully, peacefully and with love in your heart.

Those that know you by spirit will recognize you. Leave the others alone if they disturb you.

Begin to gather into your awareness all that you can concerning what it is that you should do. As time converges and begins to collapse, those of the Light frequency can band together and affect which reality you will end up with. You should know that to banish the Darkness, all that is needed is Light. You are Light, and you must begin to learn how to increase your vibration. You have learned bit by bit throughout your lifetime how to do this, but until now you probably were not aware of what you were doing.

Because you are Light, you have no doubt participated in many and various spiritual searches in an attempt to increase your vibration and thus affect your frequency. Without really knowing, you have managed to increase it enough to begin some rather amazing accomplishments. For one, if you are reading this information, you have brought us on the scene. We are converging also, so much so that we are able to slip into your reality without any problems at all. Time in our reality is so compressed that it is easy to just slip over the side, if you will, and then slip over the next one and the next. Because it may be easier for us to do this than for you to do it, we take the opportunity to in-Lighten you as to all that you are and all that you can become. Part of becoming is to realize all that you are capable of. As of now, you have a partial set of tools. As you acquire more knowledge, you add more tools. Please, make it your goal to keep adding tools every day.

Jumping now, into our dimension, there are many in this realm that do not understand or support what we do, although we know it is our destiny to travel through time and bring you this information. We are Light, such as you are Light, and we are *one* and work together throughout all layers of realities to affect the final outcome. As of now, our world is far into the future. It does not exist on planet Earth, although you and we are one and the same.

In the future, humans from Earth have migrated to other systems in the universe. Understand that life does not originate and exist solely upon Earth but begins in other places as well. All life forms are separate but interconnected and related, although appearing to be scattered throughout the universe and throughout time in varying degrees.

We, ourselves exist as more than one colony on planets in the Pleiades, although we originated from Earth aeons ago. Because of the destruction in certain time frames, humans on that path of reality learned in secret places beneath the ground how to leave behind the contamination of the Earth. Actually, the work had already begun on developing new kinds of energy that would enable humans to go far into the universe and beyond.

Please keep in mind that our past may now be your future. This might be a riddle to your mind, but think about it, continue to learn and it will become more comprehensible.

We come to tell you that the destruction of Earth does not have to be the final outcome. There are many possible realities and final outcomes, any of which you may choose. Do not believe all that you hear. Do not allow yourselves to be deceived into believing that disasters must be the end result. Fear not only controls you, but has a life of its own. As it takes shape it actually becomes a reality in its own right. It literally springs to life and wreaks havoc and destruction. Negativity perpetrates in every way possible. If you think this happens strictly in a spiritual sense where you cannot see it, all you have to do is turn on the news and listen. What is it that you hear? You hear only about that which causes you to fear. Think about it. The news is not news at all, but only negative information that has been gathered and disseminated. Its only purpose is to make you collectively afraid, thus causing mass amounts of negative energy that can be far more damaging and destructive than you could ever imagine.

Think of the negative and fearful energy of millions of people. Do you know what energy like that is capable of? It is capable of causing such destruction that you cannot begin to imagine. This negative energy can literally cause the earth to shake and rumble. It can cause winds that wipe out everything in its path, and cause mountains to erupt and rivers to overflow and spill out onto the very people that unconsciously caused the destruction.

Do you know what we are telling you? We are saying that humans possess the energy to cause the very events on Earth that cause them to tremble with fear. Even though the Earth is alive as an entity, it works in conjunction with the energy forces that inhabit it. There is great power upon planet Earth and it comes contained in the form of humans.

Chapter Nine

Transcending Time

Bringing the Light into yourself involves a rather simple technique. Because you are Light, you seek that which you are by increasing the Light of yourself. In other words, you are like a bulb that shines brighter as you keep turning the switch. Like a bright beacon in the night, your Light will shine and be obvious to all.

We speak of your Light, not as something that can be consciously observed, but as a certain vibration that is so highly tuned that it glows. There have always been the great ones throughout time that have harnessed tremendous power from the Source of all Light. As Light was their Creator, so is Light *your* Creator. Unlocking the secret of knowing who and where you belong will unlock the secret of harnessing the energy that increases your frequency. Increasing your frequency is important because in another realm it is seen as Light. What we are saying is that the spirit in each human body on Earth is capable of seeing your power and Light. Of course, on a human level these things are not acknowledged, but you will still know and feel your affect on others.

Be consciously aware of the Light. As the sun is above your head, visualize the Light above your head. Whenever you think about it, imagine this Light streaming into your body through the top of your head. You can do this wherever you happen to be, even driving down the street in your car. Imagine the Light as it pours through your body, into your arms and hands, down through your legs and feet. It is easy to fill yourself with the Light of your Creator. You have the capacity to do it simply by visualizing in whatever way works for you. Breathe it in, suck it in, pull it in, open up and allow it to pour in. We might compare the filling of Light to filling the gas tank of your car. So please, think on this, gasoline brings a car to life, as Light brings *you* to life.

Connect with your Source on a daily basis. Talk to, live with, and become one with Divineness. Begin now to think of yourself as one and the same. The principle and actions are somewhat similar with most major earthly religions, in that it is important to stay connected with that which has created you. At this time, we would like to present you with a God who does not sit in great judgment and call you wicked and evil at every turn. Perhaps you have had the experience of being told this or believing it to be true, or perhaps you have not. Nevertheless, we hope to convey to you the power of Love by your understanding that God is pure Love and is contained completely within you.

As Light, your destiny on Earth may truly be different than those around you. You will and you must experience certain circumstances, events and issues in order to find out for yourself all that you are. Some things that you experience could perhaps be looked upon as wrong or even wicked by some. Know that ultimately you possess goodness only because your source is the Light and all is working as planned.

Some of you, many in fact, will spend a lifetime migrating from place to place. This is not by accident, but by divine purpose and plan. Others will remain stationary and will not seem to want to experience even a drive to the next town. All is good and has its purpose, for most of you will be activated to perform that which you were designed for. This will happen whether you remain in one place, or whether you travel, live and work around the world. Where you find yourself is where you are suppose to be.

Each of you will have a different function to perform, a so-called mission that is your very own. You will also find each other. You will work as units and groups, and ultimately as a worldwide network of people that embody Light. More importantly, as you begin to connect with others of your kind, the frequency you produce independently will become stronger and stronger, gaining strength, until the Earth itself is covered in a web of Light energy, eventually becoming all Light. It is easy to visualize this. You can probably tell by now that we *do* like for you to visualize things. Visualization is important and powerful. Creation comes forth from the mind, for the mind is spirit and the spirit is God.

So visualize as you pull the Light into yourself. As a conduit of energy you will come alive with Light, so much so that you will become like a glowing, white candle. Visualize the Light of the flame. See it and hold it firmly in your mind. Visualize millions of others glowing around the world as each Light flickers then burns bright, the intensity of the glow spreading up and outwards until it circles the Earth. Can you see it now, the beautiful blue Earth, glowing with grids of pure, white Light?

This is what we would like to see. We call it the Gridlocking of Earth, but it will take some time to develop. As for now, a grid work of Light has begun to form. Eventually, far into the future, even going beyond where we dwell, the Earth will become as Light, and will no longer exist as a solid and physical manifestation. In other words, it only exists as it does now within a certain time period.

Perhaps another explanation would be to tell you, once again, that there is much darkness and lack of understanding at your particular sequence in time. Know that where there is such physical solidness, there will also be much darkness. What we call darkness is often simply the inability to see beyond the horizon, so to speak. It is the lack of Light, information and certain awakening. Of course, we must also stress here that to find words to explain the unseen is extremely difficult. We try with the utmost care to choose our words carefully, hoping to weave a picture in your mind of what we try to tell you. Although you are probably doing a pretty good job at grasping what we try to explain, you will not completely know or understand until you arrive at a certain evolutionary stage. This will not take place at your current level. You are in a human form and you exist in the world as it is now in that dimension of time. Although you will help to unlock the Light and let it into your world, you will still remain somewhat where you are now until you make the leap to the next level.

Your key function now is to do all you can to bring Light to the level that you exist at. It is not so important that you bring the information of what we tell you to just anyone, but that *all* those of the Light will receive what they need to further evolve themselves. Of course, you will not always be able to tell who these special ones are, and often times, you may very well be deceived. As you have been set upon your path, your level of discernment will become more finely tuned and you will be able to tell within moments if you should continue on.

Making the leap to the next level is what you should strive for, although we must say that the leap in itself is not the vital issue. It is what each one of you achieve individually, adding to the collective whole. It is the collective effort that will alter your reality, thus altering the future, thus altering all of Creation. This is what we come to tell you. Our intention is to remove the blinders and to open your eyes.

You have been walking the Earth, perhaps getting only glimpses of the entire and total truth. What you may have learned and taken into yourselves has often been very close to the truth. Know that more than likely you have been greatly deceived, especially if you have been a participant or follower of the Earth's many organized religions. You will know that what you have believed is not true when it tells you to look no further and to shut your eyes and ears to anything more. You will know it is a lie when it tells you that you are vile and wicked unless you repent, or to believe in a certain story that will relieve you of your sins in the sight of God. You will know it is untrue when what you believe offers a God that punishes and judges.

We may call the Creator by many names, even as many religions do, but know one thing for certain. The God that created you is not a God that punishes and judges. The true Creator of all is not simply a man, such as an Earthly king who sits upon a throne in all his mightiness, as those wicked and small are paraded before him. No, this is not the message we bring. Our hope is to bring you so much more. Our intent is to wake you up and shake you from your slumber. To make you think, react and act.

The God of *all* pulsates with love, brilliance and creativity, and would never think like a human being, or a Pleiadian! Even to express such an idea of a God who would punish or be unhappy with his creations for exploring and expanding their boundaries is an absurd thought at the very least. This is not the kind of God we present to you. If we are seen as evil bringers of evil things, please understand that it only seems so because we exist into the far reaches of time and come back to you with perhaps a new message.

What we tell you will not always be comprehended by the majority of those that currently live on Earth. Our message is not for the majority, but for a select few and for those that want to come fully into the Light. Although the numbers are limited, worldwide they reach into the millions. This perhaps sounds expansive, but when you consider the billions on Earth, it is few indeed.

Those of the Light are scattered across the Earth in all countries and participate in all religions. In fact, great numbers have often shrouded themselves with religion and are stuck, because as we have told you, most religions prevent further exploration. There will be some that will break away. Of course they may suffer much pain at the hands of their peers for their seemingly blasphemous ways and contrariness. We would like to tell you that these certain ones can be especially strong and powerful if they go on to the higher spiritual realms of thought and existence. They can indeed, with much perseverance and spiritual awareness, attain a level that goes far beyond what they could have ever hoped to encounter while trapped in the traditions of worldly religion.

Although there are many of the Light trapped in religions, there are many more that come from the Forces of Darkness. As we have told you about the Lesser Gods, we tell you now that many of the world's religions were formulated and plotted out by those of Darkness. As they can very well appear good and righteous, understand that in most cases, spiritually speaking, they are dark and oppressed. We are not so concerned with most humans that participate there, as this is of their choosing. We are, instead, mainly concerned for those that are blinded and trapped in that darkness, perhaps never again able to experience an original or expansive thought. So many Lights have indeed almost been extinguished.

We repeat that many of the great religions are close to the actual truth, but those of the Lesser Gods have altered the truth. Although there are many wonderful things to learn in any religion, there are also many oppressive things that are taught. This oppression originates in the Darkness, which simply means the lack of Light or information. This state instills a fear of God, a fear of evil, a fear of accepting and a fear of expanding. Because you are fearful, you will lack freedom to explore and think for yourself. Your growth will be stunted and your soul will shrivel up until your mouth only repeats what it is suppose to repeat. Of course they will call you blessed and perhaps you will smile, then do in secret all that you desire.

We are here to tell you there is more. There is more to Creation than you could possibly know. It is now that we hope you are greatly feeling the tiny sparks of recognition with what we tell you. You are coming alive with knowledge. You are growing in spirit, thus causing yourself to vibrate with a new frequency. Occasionally, you will even feel the vibration as if it is an actual physical sensation. It is not physical, but it may seem that it is. Sometimes the intensity becomes so great that things around you will seem to vibrate as well. This may disturb you because you may not understand. You may even look to others to explain the source of the vibration. We would like to tell you that this sensation is yours alone, and that no one else will know or comprehend what you are talking about.

This apparent vibration of the body is a new phenomena particular to this time sequence. Because those of the Light are being activated, this sensation is becoming felt by more and more. We want you to understand what is happening and to know and comprehend among yourselves what this is all about. It is not something as mysterious as all that. It is a perfectly rational result of rapid assimilation. To get an idea of this, think of yourself as a large machine of sorts, inputing tons of material. The process is so intense that it literally causes you to shudder.

This is your vibration; you are shuddering to the process of inputing information. You may not always be aware of this on-going process, but we assure you that it is happening on a continual basis, even as you sleep. This is so because you travel to other worlds as you are sleeping. At this point, we would like for you to know that those worlds are just as real as the one you perceive yourself to exist in now. Understand that you are capable of picking up much important information as you transcend the layers of time, which often come to you in the form of dreams. Not only do you enter these other realities continually, but you have an entirely different and often surprising relationship to people you come in contact with here. In another place, in another time, they are someone else completely, and you, while in that reality, are not the same as you are here.

You can go anywhere you want, seeing and doing whatever you please. There are people that you visit and have quite an extensive relationship with at other levels. It is also possible to visit with whom you consider to be dead in this world, but who are indeed alive in another world.

The dream world is an entirely different world than what many of you could ever know or expect. Dreams are not dreams as you think. Dreams are other places, just as this place also is a dream in another place. Understand that you are frequency that exists in all time, stretching and reaching out through eternity. If that is so, then how could you possibly remain stationary at one point? Know that you do not, but your frequency, that which we call spirit, exists all at once in all dimensions. It is in your dream world that you experience those multitudes of dimensions. They are what you call dreams.

Dreams are such that even the most preposterous one exists as a reality in another time. What you remember upon awakening is only a fraction of all that you have encountered. Please know that you are made so that you will not possibly remember all that you experience, otherwise, you could not focus on this reality.

What we say may seem like a contradiction. It may seem that we tell you to remember everything, and then we tell you that you are made so that you will not remember everything. We would like to tell you at this point, that there are a few built-in safeguards, spiritual safeguards if you will. It is important to know and be filled with information as to what you are all about, although you cannot possibly know everything at this current level. Regardless, you can accomplish much in this dream world of yours as it is. As you navigate through the corridors of time, you remember the free spirit that you are and happily you learn and grow. You will know and experience all. The only catch will be that when you return to your home, which is your sleeping body, you will not remember most of what you have seen or where you have been.

Although you do not remember, this nightly exercise is vital to your spirit. Your body, of course, is not free in this way. It is solid, immovable, inflexible and rigid. We do not have to tell you that it does not begin to navigate the invisible realm. Only your spirit can do that, and it must, and is vital to your life force. We hope that you are beginning to see how much more important your sleep is than you may have ever thought was necessary. When you go without sleep, you feel the dire consequences in your life force. In other words, you feel lifeless, do you not? Understand it is not the lack of sleep as you so think it is, but the lack of activity by your spirit in its truest and freest realm of expression.

Chapter Ten

Cosmic Energy

The triangle is an important symbol, far more important than you realize. In a triangle there are angles that are perfectly conducive for channeling and focusing cosmic energy. Scientists already know and use the triangle shape for other purposes. Although many suspect there are other rather mystical purposes, the triangle shape is still not clearly understood.

Look around and you might be surprised with the number of triangle shapes that you see. Know that in the points of the triangle, power converges. We offer the pyramids as a great and glorious example of the perfect conducer of energy. Of course we must tell you that this energy has not yet been discovered in your world, although there are those that are just now beginning to examine and explore a new kind of energy. This is a type of cosmic energy that you really know nothing about yet. It is powerful and will not be completely known in your world at the present time, although it may surprise you to know it has been used and explored in the past.

This energy can be harnessed by several methods. The triangle structure in any form is capable of harnessing great amounts of energy, as do crystals. This energy gathers and focuses at the tip or the point, creating power as it spreads downward. As of now, the mystical and the scientific properties of pyramids and crystals are vaguely known, but no one understands the vast and serious power with which these instruments and shapes are truly capable of.

We want to begin to give you information on new types of energy, as it will become important in the future, although perhaps not in your future, but in your children's. The energy with which we speak about is readily available in the very air that surrounds your planet. It is totally invisible, but it is far more powerful than anything you currently know.

When your scientists think of producing energy, they generally think in terms of something that is solid and material, something that is produced from the elements of the Earth such as water, coal or oil. Although it is known that the sun creates energy in order to produce that which fuels the Earth, the energy that we speak of is neither known nor the elements discovered. The elements are not solid nor material, but invisible, so therefore unrecognizable as something which can create usable energy. This energy can be used in an entirely different way by humans, and does not necessarily have to be harnessed in large power plants. This energy is composed from that which is around you - the sun, the stars and planets, all that surrounds you on planet Earth, including all living beings and organisms upon the planet itself. Know that what you think you can do, you can. This energy is yours to use freely, but it will take some time to realize exactly what you are capable of doing with it.

This energy, which we like to call *natural energy*, is something you can begin to use right now. You do not need to call your local energy company, nor is it something you must pay for. It is free and available to anyone, although we must tell you that not everyone will utilize that which is readily abundant.

As time moves on, there will be many that will use less reliable and accurate methods of operating and functioning in your world. Instead, they will rely more on the physical senses to accomplish what must be done, neglecting almost totally that which is available to all. We tell you now that as a direct descendant of the all pervading Source of Creation, you will know perfectly well how to activate this energy. It is the very same energy with which you were created.

Frequencies produce this energy and originate with the Prime Creator. Since all things come from the Creator, you, in essence, are cosmic energy, which is pure energy. With this, we assure you that it will be easy for you to figure out what to do once you get the hang of it. For some it will not be easy, but with learning and knowledge and awakening to the higher senses, all things will eventually come. This energy of which we speak is indeed available to all as we have said, but not all are capable of using it. You may compare this statement we make to that of a newborn baby who has all its arms and legs, but does not know what to do with them. You, dear friend, are somewhat like the new born baby. The only difference is that you *are* equipped with knowing how to use your arms and legs and much more. You only need to be activated and that is why we are here. We will help to release the knowledge that lies dormant inside of you. It has been there all along. You may have suspected it when you accomplished such feats as knowing what was going to happen, or knowing what someone was going to say, or just generally reading other people's minds.

Those of you that are capable of utilizing this energy are perhaps more sensitive than others and are sometimes accused unjustly of being *overly* sensitive. This sensitivity comes in varying levels and degrees. It can range to barely being there, to being so much there that it can interfere with your life. Let us tell you now that it will only appear to interfere. Actually, it is like a sixth sense, although it can be somewhat undeveloped or even misused or misdirected. Know that it is possible that you have some very powerful equipment. It it is simply a matter of learning how to use it.

What we are trying to tell you is that much of what you think you are, mentally or even emotionally, is not at all associated with your earthly make up. It is another more highly developed sense that is entirely dependent on that which you know nothing of. You are capable of hooking up with and utilizing an energy force which seems to lie outside of yourself, but is actually a part of yourself. If we seem to talk in circles, we are, in that we keep coming back to that which you are a part of. There is a basic theme here. You are what you were created from in the beginning. Once activated, you will project with great Light and Power all that the Creator intended for you to be.

In order to be activated, you must pay attention to everything. You must learn to be diligent in extracting the information that will empower you. How will you know what this information is? Trust us, you *will* know. If you have gotten this far with us, you certainly know by now that what you have read up to this point is what you need to start with or add to your process of in-Lightenment. Receiving the correct information is what will make you grow with knowledge. No doubt, you have been on a life long search, often with much agitation and restlessness, searching for the answers that you know lie just ahead. Your search has not been in vain. It is important that we inform you of this. Everything that you have added unto yourself has caused your Light to increase in intensity, for knowledge is power and power is Light.

Because you are Light, you may have felt as if you have often floundered throughout life, perhaps even feeling weak and inadequate because you search for those things that seem rather elusive. Know that the spiritual world only seems elusive because it is like you are on the outside trying to look in. Sometimes you cannot truly feel all that you might know and think there to be. This causes a certain emptiness in the pit of your soul, so to speak. This emptiness can create a mood. Know that it is simply that, only a mood, not to be taken too seriously, or you will get bogged down in heavy negative energy and lose your effectiveness. Understand though, that because you yearn for all that you know in your heart and soul to be, it is only natural that you will feel a certain loneliness and aching that perhaps others do not feel. Do not wallow too deeply in these feelings, otherwise you will lose your way and your purpose. With the passing of this information to you, it is certainly our hope that you are beginning to feel truly informed and your Light frequency will begin to increase its vibration.

There are other things you must do to increase your vibration. As you absorb the information we give you, you must ponder these ideas and make them your own thoughts. As you do, your mind will actually begin to transform, and our thoughts will become your thoughts because we *are* one and the same. It is our intention to elevate you to a much higher level than you currently exist at. You have the capability, but not *the know how*. We are here to give you *the know how*. This is what we planned from the beginning. You will not remember the actual planning and preparations, but know that you were there, agreeing and cooperating.

At this point, you may be thinking far too much, even trying to analyze that which cannot be logically analyzed, thus getting yourself confused and even becoming skeptical. If we are one and the same, you may ask, then how could it be that you were there as a separate entity discussing with us all the future possibilities? When we say that you were there in the beginning, know that we functioned as one and the same spirit just as we do now.

Cosmic energy permeates your being. Not only does it fill your every pore, but you are composed of it thoroughly inside and out. This is why it is easy to use and to manipulate that which you think you cannot. Many often refer to this energy as the *mind.* Think on this if you will. What exactly is the mind? Are the mind and the brain one and the same? You know the brain as gray solid matter that lies inside your skull, but ponder the mind. Some might think of the mind as the soul, but what exactly is the soul?

We tell you that the mind is energy. It is as simple as that. You have heard the saying, *Mind Over Matter.* This very short and familiar phrase tells you itself that the mind is energy. Now say it out loud, *Mind Over Matter.* This, in itself is a powerful statement, yet one you have heard over and over, so much so that it has lost its meaning *and* its power. The mind is energy. It has the power to change matter. Think on this and take it into yourself until you know it to be true. The mind is not solid gray matter, but it is the energy that pervades your being.

In this reality, your body appears to exist as something solid, although that is simply an illusion of sorts, as all matter is an illusion. The mind that you refer to is simply the power that fuels the body. In fact, it is common for many to believe the body has more substance and power than the so-called mind. This is easy to believe because you are so tuned into this frequency that it is indeed difficult to know there is anything else.

Understand that far more exists than you can possibly realize at this time. Although it may not be easy to conceive of your true potential, the energy that you possess would truly astound you. We bring you vital information, but it will be up to you to pay attention and store within yourself all that you are learning. As you do this, your mind will truly expand and you will begin to grow into all that you are. We must tell you with great happiness that you are indeed a lot more than you think you are!

If you listen, you will find us where you will. We are happy to serve as your guides. Commune with your Creator, which is at the very highest part of who you are. Visualize and pull the Light into yourself through the top of your head, as if you are a pitcher and are being filled up. You must contain this Light in all of your being without spilling it. If you do these things, your mind will indeed begin to expand, for you will have new information that will activate you to be all that you are supposed to be. Remember to always think of your mind expansion as your energy that is growing and intensifying and radiating. It is one and the same thing.

We should tell you that perhaps you will not learn all there is to learn in your life at this frequency. It is even possible that you will not be fully activated, but know that it is your duty to pass what you *do* learn to your children and to your children's children. Unto each generation the energy will increase and magnify. Because of you, all things will ultimately work for the good, but you *must* pass the information along. We have told you before, perhaps in other places, that to be Light means acquiring information. Information is vital to the evolution of Creation.

Know that it is vitally important that you learn how to manipulate *energy*. Remember, manipulating energy is simply mind over matter. Knowing how to do this will be crucial as time moves forward and converges. You must learn to operate and function with true power, perhaps not to the fullest degree yet, but at least to some degree. You must pass what you know to your children because they are still fairly new to the Earth plane and it will be easy for them to accept what you teach them. Because they will learn quickly, their energy will become activated, thus making them effective at an earlier age to do that which they were designed for.

It is most likely that you have learned what you know at a later time in life, thus making it more difficult for you to believe and practice what you know. You have been bogged down in negative energy for many years, with perhaps no one at all to in-Lighten you or show you the way. You now know the way partly and can help to Light the path. It is totally up to you. How hard and diligent you work will make a difference as to how effective you will become. Please remember though, it *is* important that you teach your children, and in turn, they will teach their children and this will open up places that you had no idea existed.

What you teach and show the younger generation will increase, intensify and magnify many times over and will definitely affect the future. This is why we believe it is vital to come to you at this time. Without Light, all is hopeless and the future may possibly hold disaster and tragedy. Although tragedies cannot be fully and completely avoided in all possible realities, they certainly can be changed from terrible destruction to things much more manageable when Light has been activated. Light is *knowing*, and *knowing* will enable you to choose your circumstances, thus changing and affecting your future reality.

Reaching Beyond

It would surprise many of you to know there are actual planetary beings living among you. We must tell you that Earth is certainly a diverse enough planet that multitudes can come here and integrate without any problem at all. There are various species that come from many places. Often it is simple to take on the human form, although there are intelligences that take on whatever form they choose. As of yet, Earthly humans have not evolved enough to know to whom or to what they speak. It is not always a matter of what something or someone looks like, as they can look perfectly human, animal or plant like. Know that it is always by using the senses that differences will be felt and noticed, although not always at a conscious level.

As we have told you, many species are born unto the Earth, meaning they have been reincarnated into human form. They were born from a human female body as a baby and continue to evolve as human. Know indeed, though, as incredulous as it may sound, creatures in the shape and form of humans have originated in many places in the universe. When we tell you that planetary beings exist in your world now, we are saying that they have arrived from other places and attempt to integrate themselves into Earth's society. There are reasons that this is done; the biggest reason being is to gather information.

Earth is full of information that is valuable to other worlds and to other species. There are many ways of assimilating and gathering this information, some of which are known, but most are unknown. We must inform you, though, that much activity by alien species goes unnoticed or is ignored. Not only is it ignored, but it is simply not taken seriously by most of humankind. This is a problem not totally caused by human fault or error, but by the heavy negative energy force that encompasses Earth. This energy force is such that it is comparable to an almost solid shield of darkness. It is designed to blind and trap you into a very narrow view of the way things are. Without this controlling factor, humans would figure it all out and things would be very different on Earth. Those of the Light would not be blinded anymore. Instead, they would be free to do that which they were designed for. As it is now, many Light creations that reside upon Earth know nothing of their true purpose. Instead, they stumble blindly in the dark, searching forevermore for their grand purpose in life, which *always* seems to elude them.

Alien beings come in many forms. Some appear very, very solid, some are tiny, and some are large, ugly or even beautiful. We tell you that most will never appear in their true form, but can and do transform into that which will allow them easy access into your world without attracting undue attention. Some of these beings work directly with humans and some work between the layers of human consciousness. As much as we regret having to tell you, there are many motives, some of which are not so good and others that have a purpose, which you may interpret as divine. You may even interpret *our* intent and purpose as divine, as we work most often in the sub-conscious or between the layers of human consciousness.

If you think of us as rather divine like, we must tell you that, *yes*, our purposes and intentions may indeed go beyond the human scope, but we are not truly divine in the sense that our original Creator is divine. There are other beings that exist at a much higher level than us and can be perceived as angelic or God like. Actually, upon thinking about it, many beings past the Earth realm level have been perceived as God like!

Know that we come to you with a purpose and that we do so in love. This love with which we speak is nothing you can know or comprehend at your present moment. This is a love that is completely devoid of greed, hate, selfishness and evil. There is only one true intention and that is to inspire and further the creation. As of yet, such complete love does not currently exist at the human level.

Even as you read this, it is difficult for you to fully grasp that which we speak because you are shrouded completely in a thick fog, all memory of your original creation forgotten and all memory of anything real and divine forgotten. Yes, we call the spiritual world *real* instead of the one you exist in now. Your Earth is simply an illusion in the overall scheme of things. You know this to be true in your heart. That is why you may often feel a distant, aching longing in the deepest part of yourself. It is your spirit trying to reach beyond the fog to what it once knew.

We come to you now to help you remember all that was and all that should be. As you begin to awaken, your job will be to take what you know to others. Do not be concerned with those that laugh and scorn you. Move away, and move on, for they are the lost ones. *They* are not of the Light and they will naturally try to dissuade you. Know that you are strong. It is important that you not shrink back and be thwarted from what you know in your heart you must do. We are always there, helping you to help others. At this time, please try to remember and know that we have been with you a long, long time. Start to think on your life and begin to remember all the strange little things that have gone on. Have you not spent a lifetime feeling different than others, perhaps? Have you not felt strange, or have others not called you weird, laughing as they told you so? Know now, that you *are* different. *You* are the Light and you *are* special. It will be possible for you to accomplish amazing things. Not only will the Light of your being cut a path in front of you, but it will shine a bright spotlight on just the right paths, guiding you through the jungles of affliction, pain and suffering. Your Light will always lead you in the way you should go.

You must begin to fine-tune your senses. As you do, you will develop the capacity to know Light from Dark. It is very important to know what is good and what is bad. There are those who will never develop the ability to discern, but you have the equipment. All you have to do is listen to your heart. Knowing things is not always a matter of the intellect. There are plenty of smart people around, but they often operate by intellect instead of intuition. As it is now, intellect is valued highly in what you call civilized and developed countries, while intuition is not always accepted or taken so seriously.

We tell you it is by intuition that the most important elements are to be found. There are humans who have lived, and are living now, that know the value of intuition. These people are not always valued or thought of very highly because of their seeming lack of civilized behavior or sophistication. Regardless of their outward appearance, they are far superior in that they are able to operate at a level that many are not capable of. Once these levels are obtained, the physical and material things of this world become less important.

There are entire civilizations living now that operate at a different frequency. We tell you that many of them are creations of the Light. They often live in groups or clusters and are scattered across the world in many nations, such as Africa, Australia, India, South America, many islands, and even in North America. Sometimes these groups are so isolated that they are practically unheard of, or else not much attention is paid to them. More often than not, civilized nations look down their noses, if you will, thinking these people lack the intelligence to even care for themselves properly. The truth is, these people serve a higher purpose in the world than anyone might suspect. As an isolated group, or culture unto themselves, they serve as a special unit that is unified for the purpose of creating and intensifying Light upon Earth.

Now, imagine if you will, each one of these people as a very tall pole that is sparking with Light and energy. The sparks fly so high that they touch the next pole, and the next, and the next, until the very air above and between *all* the poles come alive with electrified energy. Will this energy not have the power to change the very molecules in the air? This air space can definitely become different, and although you may not always understand the deeper nature of the changes, it *is* being changed.

Those of the Light that cluster together have tremendous power to affect the Earth. Many of these special people throughout history have realized their purpose in one way or another, but many have not, especially in modern times. There are millions that are still searching for their purpose in life. They grasp and clutch at the wrong things and suffer tremendously from disappointment and heartache. When finally they achieve what they thought they wanted to achieve, only emptiness and lack of satisfaction fills the soul with bitter disillusionment.

We want to tell you there is more, so much more that *you* are suppose to be accomplishing. You know this to be so and that is why perhaps you are reading this with eager anticipation. You would not have read this far if you were not of the

Light. You would not be here now if you did not
know in your heart that you belong here. You
would not continue reading if you did not believe
in the very deepest part of yourself that we have a
message especially for *you.*

You are *not* weak because you stay with us.
You are *not* trying to escape reality. Do not believe
it when they try to tell you that you are. You are
not reading this book because you are a strange
and weird person. You are simply here with us
because this is where you are suppose to be. Think
of it as a pre-arranged meeting. You marked it on
your calendar so long ago that you have forgotten
and we are simply calling you up to remind you.
We will jog your memory and you will at long last
remember the things that we are telling you. In
fact, understand that what we tell you now, will
become yours to know forever.

You are connected to others, not in the
physical realm, but in the spiritual realm, which
you may very well think of as the unseen realm.
You have heard of collective consciousness. We
tell you that indeed there is such a thing. We tell
you it is true that you may not be the first person
to think of an idea. If you think of it, no doubt
someone else has thought of it too. This occurs
because consciousness is one. All consciousness
is the consciousness of the ultimate Creator God.
This may be a difficult thought to fathom, but
think of all minds throughout all of time as one

mind. This one mind is that of the Great Spirit, the only Spirit that has created everything under creation. When you think, know that you are thinking the thoughts of God. Every time you act, know that your expression is the expression of God. Think on this, if you will, by taking a moment to reflect or meditate on what we have just told you.

If your thoughts are the thoughts of God, does this make you a God? Yes, we all are a portion or fragment if you will, of the Spirit. If we are fragments, this means we are a part of God, does it not? The great religions on Earth tell you that you were created by God, but this is only a simplified version of who you really are. We are here to tell you that *all* consciousness *is* God. This is not to say that you have the same or equal power with the prime Creator, but know that the Creator is part of you and you are a part of the Creator. You are one and the same, as *all* of creation is.

If you have the mind of God, then all things should be possible for you, should they not? If the Creator did all that the Creator did, then should we not be able to do the same? We say to you that, yes, *all* things should be possible, but all is *not* possible, at least not everything at your point in time. We *do* want to stress to you that all *could* be possible in your current reality, but there are certain laws and patterns to everything. Just as physical creation evolves, so does the spiritual. As all time exists at the same time, many things extend beyond reality as you know it into other realities and on into the future. Many things that you currently believe are impossible *are* possible. They are taking place precisely at this moment in realities that run parallel to your own.

You experience these other realities in your dreams. If you dream of flying, then believe that you have actually flown. Many of you have such memories of flying, but are unable to insert these memories into your current idea of reality. Because you think flying is impossible, it is. We want to point out most whole-heartedly that there *are* realities in which you fly. Flying is not the impossible task that you believe it to be. In fact, we tell you that nothing is really impossible, as all matter is simply the gathering of frequency. Frequency is movable and penetrable, and is capable of great ranges of flexibility.

On a higher level yet, frequency, in simple terms, is nothing more than the thought waves or patterns of the Original Creator, which in essence is pure Spirit. Just imagine what you could do if you were a dream and had the flexibility to move about unencumbered without a physical body or physical reality. You could certainly achieve anything you wanted. If you wanted to fly, you would simply do it. As you thought it, so would you do it.

Yes, we tell you now, that as you think, so can you do it. *Nothing* is impossible. As Spirit thinks things into being, so can you think things into being. Although we tell you these things, we know that it will take most of you a lifetime, and maybe never, to assimilate and learn to do what you *think* is impossible. Although we realize this, we still come to tell you that the way must be prepared, not only for yourself, but also for the future generations. As you gain Light and knowledge, so will your children begin to learn, and your children's children, and their children.

As you take in higher learning you must know now that you will be activated to achieve all that you have learned. As you do so, your body will actually begin to evolve and you will pass this to future generations not only in a spiritual way but through the physical as well. Your physical structure through your DNA is continually changing and evolving to accommodate that which happens first in the spiritual realm. In other words, in places that are unseen to you as of yet.

Know this to be true, how you develop spiritually *will* have a direct impact on your physical body. Your body *will* grow and develop to accommodate the spiritual. We do not always mean to say that your body will necessarily change its outward characteristics, but its internal structure is where the most profound changes will take place.

Understand that you will not automatically sprout wings in order to fly, but that flying is simply a matter of thought. In time, it will be possible to think yourself right through a wall and up a flight of steps in two seconds if that is what you want.

Look at us. We say this with a smile, but are we not a good example? We speak to you, yet we are not in your physical world. Have we not achieved the absolute impossible by speaking within the hearts and minds of people? How do we do this? It is easy for us as we live far into your future and have evolved to this point, as you will begin to do so now. We can simply think our way into other realities. In other words, you exist in our dreams and all we do is insert ourselves into you as we dream together. Remember, we are your future and you are our past. In our dreams we exist as one. If we exist as one, then we can function as one. Although we function as one, we are really not one, but separate because we are the future extension of *you.* As we reside within you, outside of you and in the future, we have certainly developed and gone past the Earth realm mode. We have evolved to this level and so it is easy for us to accomplish that which we come to tell you.

You probably will not be able to walk through walls any time soon, but now that you have this information you will begin to think about it. As you do, you will begin to evolve. As of now, you can do your part by beginning to practice and visualize the information we impart to you. Visualization is very important at your level as it helps you to evolve and awaken. By visualizing, you can begin to actually change things. You have no doubt discovered this in some areas of your lives. Or maybe you have not always realized by your very thoughts that you have indeed changed things. So it is that we must tell you, perhaps even warn you, that thoughts are powerful. Not only are thoughts powerful, but words are just as powerful.

Know that as you think, so shall it be. Thoughts, and even more so, repeated thoughts and even words have the power to change things. Take a look at how and what you think. What does your mouth proclaim over and over? Are you not making your own truths? How many times do you hear the phrase, *I'm getting old*? Do people not *cause* themselves to become old by their repeated thoughts and words? Starting today, become aware of your thought patterns. Examine the things you say. Take note of how many times you repeat the same things. Think about what is happening in your life. Are you directing your life down a negative path by uttering the same negative words all the time?

How about your children, your family and friends? What do you tell them repeatedly? Above all, we hope that everything you say is both beneficial and positive to their growth as well as to their spiritual evolvement. Think on this, if you tell your children repeatedly that they cannot do something, will they go through life believing that indeed they cannot? You have the power and ability to form thoughts and beliefs in other people by what you utter. Be careful that you bring not only encouragement and inspiration to your children, but to all those around you. *You* are Light and it is your duty to pass out correct information without condemnation.

Begin to speak of those things which are not ordinarily spoken of, such as flying for instance. Begin slowly and cautiously if you are not sure. We understand that you will most likely get some strange looks, but you will endure and you will go on with that which you know and were put here for. Although you may experience a bit of uncomfortableness, you knew this would happen from the beginning. Believe us when we tell you it was really a minor detail that you did not worry about at all. You may worry now because what you see appears as solid and real. You have learned to embrace it so much so that you grip it firmly and hold on tight.

You have not been able to see clearly because your usual consciousness has been shrouded in a thick mist. The mist has swirled about you, tricking and deceiving you throughout your lifetime. Only in rare moments have you been able to catch a glimpse of that which you know to be. Perhaps in the quieter moments of your deepest self, you have even sensed the mysteries of the universe. Or maybe it is that you have instantly clamped yourself shut whenever you begin to think too much on spiritual matters, as if you are committing a grave sin by delving further into the mysteries.

We tell you that it is your right to dig deeper and to find out all there is to know. It is nonsense to believe any religion that tries to tell you it is wrong when you are hungering and want to know more. We tell you that it is *not* wrong for you to be curious and to explore. There are those of you who have never been much into religion, but there are *many* more that have been greatly influenced by what your so-called Holy books have told you. We say to you that not all is as Holy as you may believe. Much of what you have been led to believe has only been designed to keep you in ignorance.

At this time we realize that many of you may remain skeptical and untrusting, even as you read and absorb our words. There has been much material about the spiritual realm. It may be that you have problems with *what* exactly to believe in. Therefore, we put forth the question, why would you believe something that tells you to stop your search? Why would you believe that which limits you and puts you in bondage and fear to explore any further? We tell you that to explore and search out the answers is the ultimate freedom and the way to find the truth. We tell you that you should never, never limit yourself, not even to all that *we* tell you. The spiritual realm contains so much that it would be impossible to learn it all in one lifetime. Simply know that it exists and it is very real. It is a large part of *who* you are, and *who* you are is very special and very important.

Cosmic Cohesiveness

You are interconnected to all that is. Know that whatsoever you think, others will think also. Not only are you connected at this level of reality, but you are connected on many, many levels. What you may perceive as *your* thoughts may very well be the thoughts of another. At this time you do not realize the immensity of your connectedness. Know that you are not a world unto yourself, but please think of all human consciousness as a huge pool of never ending proportions.

We have told you many times that it is possible for your consciousness to go out in all directions. Not only does it take place while you are sleeping, but while you are awake as well. Have there not been times in your life when you encountered strange moments? Perhaps there have been those moments when you have felt that what you were experiencing has happened before. You call this phenomenon *Deja Vu*, although no one really has an adequate explanation for it. We tell you that it is a consciousness switch that you recognize in its most subtle form, yet you have no idea how or what has really happened. Your consciousness has jumped ahead to a slightly different reality, which exists only seconds, or perhaps minutes ahead of the one in which you are in at the moment. So, you may experience the exact same thing you experienced only seconds ago, especially if the circumstances or activity in your reality is the same as in the other reality.

When you take a moment to think about it, it is most likely that you remember other strange and unexplainable phenomenon that has occurred throughout your lifetime. What we are speaking of here is phenomenon of the conscious mind, not necessarily in your physical realm or space, although you may experience physical symptoms when you experience any kind of change in your consciousness. You may experience dizziness or other sensations such as feeling elongated, large or small. Perhaps you have felt *not really here*, or have even had heightened states of awareness, or a seemingly very alone feeling. There are many sensations that the physical senses are capable of feeling when a switch in consciousness has taken place. Please know that you *are* constantly switching realities. Of course we tell you this is not a very well known fact in your world, but it is true nevertheless.

You switch realities quite easily, although you probably are not aware of it. There *are* those that have become sensitive and have learned to be aware of what their consciousness is doing. Know that when we talk about consciousness, we are talking about spirit. There have been, and the numbers are ever increasing, people that travel in the spirit and remember the details. You perhaps call these spiritual journeys, astral projection or astral travel. This is a good name, as the spirit does indeed travel on the astral plane so to speak.

We would like to remind you again that the spirit does not actually leave the body, but already exists throughout all of time. This will no doubt be a new concept for many to grasp. We tell you again that it only seems like you travel, but think on this for a moment, if you will. Imagine a string stretched out for one mile and this string is your soul that exists from the beginning of time to the very end of time. Throughout your total existence, your lives, which you may simply refer to as realities, are located at varying points on the string. To experience a particular reality, you focus on one. It will appear to be the only one, when in actuality you simply do not remember the others. Anytime you focus on one reality, you will only know and experience *that* one, as if it is the only one that exists. All others will be forgotten for the moment, unless of course your perceptions have been heightened, and then you will be capable of seeing into places that perhaps others do not.

The effects of perceiving other realities will often change the very nature of who you are. Your personality and character will seem to change from day to day. Often you will not understand why you are the way you are. As people and events bleed through, you may become bewildered with the input. Not only will you worry and see yourself as unstable, but others may see you that way as well. You will be left with definite impressions, sometimes vague, but nevertheless clear in that you know they do not fit with this life or reality as you perceive them.

This bleeding through of other realities may disturb some. It is only because they are becoming sensitive to all that is, which causes their consciousness to expand, but they may lack the necessary information to utilize all they are experiencing. That is why we are here. Our hope is to bring new and vital information. You and many others are now beginning a new journey down a path that will grow brighter with each new step. The only difficult part for some is opening up to new ideas. Shedding Light in the dark corners of your mind will reveal things you never even imagined. Do not be afraid, even if others are afraid to walk with you. Not only is this a new journey, but it is a new path. Although it has been walked before, it has never been walked by you. Along this path, you will discover things about yourself that you never knew. You will be astounded that what you thought was rigid is not rigid at all, but is very flexible. You can go as far as you want. The choice is yours and yours alone. We are only here to help you. We will never force you. There is a Divine Creator far beyond us, and even then you will not be forced to go where you do not choose to go.

Know that you sprout from a Prime Creator, therefore, you are simply an expression of divine thought. Whatsoever the Creator thinks, you will think. Whatsoever the Creator would like to know and experience, you will also know and experience. At this point, do not be alarmed and feel as if you have no control over your own destiny. All creations are an extension of the Creator's so called thought processes. Therefore, all are intertwined and work together to affect each other. Nothing in the universe is haphazard, but everything works together to create cosmic cohesiveness. There is a divine plan and in the end all will have worked together for the ultimate good.

Know now that nothing is by accident. All has been created and put into action for a purpose. We tell you that a system exists upon Earth in which all things appear as one thing, but are indeed quite another thing. Flip a coin and on one side there is a view of something and on the other side the scene completely changes. What you see is not what you think it is. Take the clouds for instance. They appear as big wads of cotton stretched and puffed across your sky. This image is perfectly accepted by all humans, is it not? In other words, the sky is taken for granted. The sky is blue and is suppose to have clouds. After all, this is what you have been seeing for as long as you can remember.

We do not mean to surprise you or shock you, but know that this is the only view that has been presented up until now. We are here to flip the coin and make you see something else. And so it is that we tell you the clouds are not what you may think they are. They are not at all condensed vapor as you presume they are, but are more like condensed energy, which only appears as vapor in your reality. This particular kind of energy emanates from all living things such as plants, animals, water, even rocks, and yes, most of all, human beings. Humans create much energy because of their emotions.

Most of you would never suspect that you were capable of creating clouds. In fact, it is perfectly normal to believe that weather originates from anything other than humans. After all, weather, as you perceive it, is rather ordinary, but we tell you now that it is indeed *very* far from ordinary. The truth is, humans along with other living organisms generate the energy that creates molecular changes in the air structure surrounding Earth. Of course, all this is done without any conscious knowledge whatsoever that it is happening. Once again it is a phenomenon that takes place without your input or control, such as your heartbeat or the breathing of air. Although you do not realize at this time that weather is generated by you, it is a well know fact at other levels of consciousness. It is at those levels where collective consciousness works to control and stabilize not only the weather but the forces of the Earth as well.

Know that all things are made of energy, which although is invisible, creates a moving, living and powerful force. Therefore, it would make perfect sense that so much energy created by so many living organisms would have the capacity to move, grow, circulate and affect the very space in which you live and work. The winds, rain, the snow, the humidity, even natural disasters, are all created by energy from living things.

As energy emanates from living organisms, it also affects your planet. The Earth itself is a living, thriving organism. It is connected as one with all other living things. As you feel, so does the Earth feel. Take mass living consciousness and the energy created from it, and this energy is enough to indeed cause planetary changes such as earthquakes. In fact, earthquakes are indeed intensifying as human energy intensifies. Human energy is intensifying simply because there are major transitions taking place. As transitions happen, emotions are heightened and become powerful enough to literally *move* the Earth.

Yes, there are always the scientific details that people like to point out, such as the faults and mantle plates beneath the Earth that are believed to shift and change and cause Earthquakes. This of course is a simple explanation to explain why the Earth rumbles and shakes like it does. Know that this in itself would not cause the Earth to move as rocks cannot move of their own accord. It takes some kind of energy to move the immobile things that exist upon and within the Earth. Try now to grasp and hold onto the concept that human emotions are extremely powerful. It is this highly concentrated form of energy, which can make the Earth literally move.

We have told you this for a reason. Believe now, that it is time you must begin to fathom and understand what you are really capable of. One human has power, but many, many humans have unlimited power. There are those outside of your realm that know this and use it to their advantage. Negative emotions can become rampant simply by injecting fear into your Earthly culture. This happens on a constant and daily basis and humans have no idea what is going on as they glue themselves enmasse before their television sets.

Just think of the emotions of millions around the world as they view the nightly news. The energy of the multitudes induced by one negative news event would be enough to generate hurricanes, earthquakes and countless other disasters. We do not want to dishearten you by telling you this energy only creates havoc, but understand now that it does indeed cause *all* normal weather and Earth related patterns and conditions.

The problem is, that without knowledge of what you are doing, emotions run amuck and cause the very thing to happen that you do not want to happen. Know that emotions are powerful. Emotions can make things happen. Negative emotions can be just as powerful as positive emotions. *You* that are of the Light can choose that which will enable you to effectively change reality itself. It is so very easy to get yourself bogged down in the events that surround you. Beware, friend, for you are very capable of sinking into the mud with the rest if you allow yourself to become part of this all pervading drama.

Please, understand that although you seem to get caught up in your scenarios as you perceive them to be happening, it is possible for you to remove yourself *emotionally*. Now, perhaps you believe that by removing yourself emotionally you would no longer be able to participate in life as fully as you might think you should. We do not want you to misunderstand. We tell you now that emotion is definitely a good and beneficial thing as we have told you before. It *always* connects you to those spiritual areas outside of yourself. The problem we see though, is that you have a tendency to get caught up in Earthly dramas so much so that you forget what your real intent and purpose is. From our perspective, we see that you are capable of enjoying even the negative events without even realizing consciously what you are doing.

This is what concerns us, for you forget so easily why it is that you entered into your particular time sequence. We understand *why* you forget, and it is not your fault at all. It is as if you are trapped in the web of a spider. As you continuously struggle to escape, you forget what you were suppose to be doing in the first place. This is why we are here, to speak to certain individuals around the world so they can bring the message for all who are suppose to hear. Be assured that you *will* hear our voice and it *will* begin to activate your memory as to your *real* purpose on Earth.

We are the Pleiadians and although we come from the Pleiades, we are also your future. We know things that are impossible for you to know at this time. We know these things because we have already seen the possible realities. We come to help you choose a better reality, not only for yourselves, but also for us and for all of Creation.

Perhaps you are aware that many indigenous people of the world are direct descendants of those that originated in other places in the universe, or perhaps you did not know this until just now. But, yes, we tell you that many humans that have populated the Earth have been scorned and ridiculed and hated. Know that they as well as their legends are indeed based in fact. It would behoove *you* of the Light - *you* who crave spiritual information - *you* who are looking toward the Heavens for something divine, to start learning something of your heritage as well as that of other people. You may be surprised when you discover that your descendants have not originated from the Earth as you once thought, but are from other star systems.

You may suddenly find that you have been wrong in your thinking as to the origins of humankind. If you have any Native American Indian blood or Asian, please know that it is more than likely that your heritage is in the stars. This physical tie within your DNA is what may have stirred you to search for your real identity. If you do not especially identify with us, yet still search for what you do not quite understand, know that the Earth has been populated with beings from many other places, You may originate from that which you know not. We would like to console you and tell you not to give up Hope. Many beings from many places have indeed been friends over the ages and will continue to be friends, even within the bodily guise of humans while on Earth. Is it not wonderful that we can all learn from one another? But yet, while we invite you to stay and partake of our knowledge, we understand that you may have to end this search and begin a new one elsewhere. We would like to tell you that it is very possible now, in this time frame, to find what you are looking for. Never give up. Continue to search until you feel satisfied. Find the path on which you must tread. Do the work with which you were designed for. There is purpose unto all Creation and each of you were designed with great and unlimited purpose.

Chapter Thirteen

Manifesting in the Physical Realm

You are one with all. Know this to be true. As the wind blows and the sun shines and the trees bend, you, also, are part of the fabric that is woven as one into your world. Although you appear to exist in time as you know it, and have inserted yourself into the physical reality of Earth as it is now, in essence, you do not exist at all as you may think you do. This may seem to be a contradiction, but let us explain further.

Know that all matter only appears as solid, when actually it is frequency that vibrates at different levels or tunes, if you will. Each and everything that you perceive in your world is nothing more than this. Nothing is solid, nothing is material, nothing is physical, but everything is indeed as a puff of smoke. We do not mean to dishearten you, quite the contrary. It is our hope only to in-Lighten you. Perhaps it is so that you wonder why we tell you such things, after all, why must you know these things? Believe us when we say to you that everything we tell you is to your highest benefit and in time you will come to know this is true.

To know that all is not as you perceive it to be is to understand how to maneuver more accurately in your time space. With more exactness, you will be capable of acting and reacting with greater speed, knowledge and wisdom. What we give you are the divine keys so that you can become much more effective concerning the job you are here to do.

To tune your mind to a higher conscious level, it is important that you begin to access that which is within you. We are not talking of physical organs, such as the brain and the heart, but that which is spirit. Up until now, you perhaps have relied way too much on your mental faculties, not that this is wrong, but understand that the mind and the spirit are two entirely separate things. The mind springs forth from the brain, which is purely a physical function of the body. We are not saying the brain is useless for indeed it serves a great and noble cause. It is what enables you to operate coherently in a very physical and material world. You *need* your physical brain and the spirit of your mind working in conjunction with each other in order to be able to do this.

The brain is not often fully understood, even by your scientists. In fact, some have even speculated that perhaps the soul lies coiled within the brain as if the brain were only a long and hollow tube. Of course there has only been speculation up to this point. No one, as of yet, has been able to produce any evidence that the soul is made of such substance or that it could even be housed or encased, if you will, inside the confines of a human brain.

Your soul or spirit does indeed dwell within you, but know that it is not coiled inside your brain or even housed inside your body, as you might perceive it to be. Your spirit is divine, meaning that it emanates from the original Creator. It pours forth, such as Light pours from the sun. Light is actually invisible, is it not? You are able to see that the day is brightened, but you cannot see that the light streaming in the air around you is of any particular substance. It is not solid or liquid or vapor. As you look beyond and into the distance, you can see that it is day, but can you look at the air in front of you and see the Light? Of course you can see it, but can you touch it, feel it, grasp it and hold it?

Ponder this but for one moment, and as you do, think of your Spirit. Your Spirit is the driving force behind all that you do, especially as a worker in the Light. Know that you are driven by Spirit. It will brighten you and Light the way. People will actually be able to see that you are different. You *are* special and you *are* the Light, but they will no more be able to touch and feel and grasp your Spirit than they can touch the sunshine.

Accessing your Spirit, or tuning into your Soul, only requires that you understand and realize the *divine nature of who you are.* You are not a clump of clay devoid of Spirit. Know that what you are is because of your Spirit. Your body and Spirit have become one, fused together, but at the same time think of your body as if it were riding on a wave. Immediately, you may think of a surfer. This is fine if it will help you to visualize, but instead of water, imagine the wave is composed of cosmic frequency. You are a ball of Light bouncing through time, riding the Cosmic Wave. The Light that you are is the Spirit of *all* that you are. What you think you are, you are not at all.

The key to accessing your Spirit lies within you. All you have to do now is begin to turn the key. Dare to walk through the door of your spiritual mind and see what is on the other side. As you allow yourself to peer into this new world, you will begin to remember that which you originated from. You will begin to see that you are not solid and rigid at all like you once perceived yourself to be. Even your dramas that you participate in are not as solid as you may think them to be. Your Spirit originates with the highest frequency, which is the ultimate frequency, and which is the Creator of all. You begin with God and ride through time like a never ending, golden thread of Light. You unravel throughout eternity, twisting, touching and zigzagging in and out of what you call realities, or lives.

We will help you to turn the key and unlock the secrets. It is then when you will begin to truly know and understand that there is no such thing as death. How can death possibly exist when your Spirit so obviously traverses the Cosmos with such joy, abandonment and freedom? The Spirit is never ending. Know this to be true without doubt. The Spirit *never* dies. It is as free as the wind. As you think you die, know that the Spirit is leaping and springing forth from the shackles of human bondage instead. There is never ending joy to its final escape into that which it came. This is the true home from which we all were created, and from which we all will continue to reside in.

We do not mean to portray such a gloomy picture of Spirit within body, but understand that to experience certain frequencies is indeed an adventure in itself. Always remember that life in the more solid and physical form is something the Spirit chooses. Nothing is by accident, and nothing is hurled randomly into the Earth realm. All is by careful choice and by expert planning. There is a reason and purpose to all things. To be human is to know and understand only those lessons that can be learned at a lower frequency

143

level. The lessons learned will help to toughen you, so to speak, and will enable you to elevate to higher realms. This is the natural order of things. As the progression of a human life from birth to death contains many lessons, so it is that the soul's progression contains many lessons.

It is vital that you understand that Divine Light is Love, for without Love you understand nothing. Know that love is the essence of all. You have absolutely nothing without it, and in nothing you will experience the absence of all that is good. Knowing love is a matter of being finely tuned to the higher spiritual forces. What you call love is often times only a yearning for love. Since you may have difficulty finding the true spiritual essence of real love, you oftentimes mistake feelings of lust for love. Love and lust are not the same. We hope you already know that. If you ever hope to find a truer form of real love, then you must begin to attune yourself to a higher dimension. It is only there that real love can manifest. Do not be unnecessarily unhappy with this thought and begin to think you will never know love. Although the higher dimensions translate into love, it is possible as you evolve spiritually to access that love and plant it within yourself.

We radiate goodwill towards you always. We strive continuously to bring a message that will strengthen you for battle, for the life that you have chosen is indeed a battleground. There are ways to fight and ways to endure. Know now that the battle is not yours alone. There is the Spirit within you, and we offer ourselves as well.

The information that we give you will help to rearrange the molecules within you. If this sounds like a difficult task, it is not at all, as molecules are only the minute particles that create a sense of reality. We say *sense of reality* because reality itself is only an illusion. Before you toss this aside, we want you to know that we all participate in the illusion for a reason. Nevertheless, setting illusions aside, we would now like to speak of the rearrangement of your molecules. As we impart knowledge to you, we hope you will begin to see how rearranging your molecules would be an easy task to perform, especially when molecules do not exist in the first place. Please meditate on this but do not try to figure it out at the moment. Instead we ask that you concentrate on the perceived solidness of your reality and work within that framework.

Now imagine, if you will, billions of molecules massing together in empty space. They are forming and bunching into various clumps that soon begin to take shape. After a period of time they begin to look like a human. These molecules appear as tiny round balls and are extremely movable. So if that is the case, would it not be easy to simply move them around as energy forces come along and blow them into various shapes sizes? This is precisely what is happening as your molecules are blasted and blown into a different form. Of course, you are not going to look into your mirror and see a totally different person than what you were, but the changes will be noted as you indeed begin to evolve and change. It is important that you understand how these internal changes will not be seen, but they will definitely be felt. As your DNA structure code is changed, you will change. As your nervous system is changed, you will also be changed. Many systems will begin to alter as you begin to alter. As a result, you may experience so called symptoms of many kinds. These symptoms are really only a minor annoyance compared to the final and glorious overhaul of your entire system. We hope to give you assurance by telling you that it is possible that you will only grow better as the years go by. In fact, some will marvel that you do not seem to age or deteriorate as others do.

Your structures, both internal and external, will not wear as a normal human does, for you have been re-tuned. Think of what can be done with a computer to make it more powerful. More chips, more circuitry, expansion, perhaps better speakers and a better monitor. The same can be done for the human body, although your traditional medicine knows very little about the body as a spiritual entity. Traditional Western medicine approaches healing from a strictly physical perspective, totally eliminating what is really important to the healing of the body.

To truly heal the body is to know how to access that which is beyond the physical. There are parts of the body that are truly invisible but that are known by some. Many of the more ancient forms of medicine, and that which is known to indigenous people are far more accurate in that they heal and cure that which is invisible. The invisible are those parts that are spiritual and vibrate to a higher frequency. It is that which keeps you grounded physically. By dealing only with the physical and ignoring the spiritual, much harm is done in that healing is not complete. All true healing begins with the spiritual and not with the physical. First, you sprout in the spiritual realm and *then* the physical. To reverse the order is unnatural, and can do nothing but cause damage. Know this to be true. The physical body cannot be healed alone and apart from the soul. To do so only mends a portion while neglecting the whole.

Chapter Fourteen

Instruction in the Light

We have opened you up. We have been fine-tuning you, adjusting your frequency, if you will. As we load information into you, you will find that you will experience deep and profound changes. These changes will eventually connect you back to the place you originated from, for your true home is not of this world.

We are giving you certain information, which will enable you to navigate more successfully within the time frame that you find yourself at. You may not always realize or even accept that you are taking in and storing information. Believe us when we tell you this information will help to restore and further your functions at all levels. You will become what you were meant to be. Not only will we speak to you within these pages, but you will also encounter others that will remind you and even extol you to see and become that which you were designed for.

We work with Spirit always. We would like to remind you of that just so you will be assured that we do not come alone and work independently of our Creator who has created all. Know that we have one and the same Creator.

Religion as you know it will blind you to the absolute truth. Understand that what we tell you will open you up to encompass all of God as God was meant to be known. We call God by many names, as we realize there are indeed many names that our Divine Creator goes by. As we have mentioned before, God is neither a he nor a she, but is frequency existing at the highest order. There is really no name in the human scheme of things to describe the glory of this certain frequency that begins and ends in all things. Although we would like to present a name, which we feel would truly describe the divine aspects of our Creator, we find no name except that which is familiar to you. The name of *God* denotes a divine deity to some, while to others, another name entirely would conjure up diviness. It is irrelevant what you choose to call the highest and most divine deity, but what *is* important is that you know and understand the aspects of deity.

Imagine yourself as an empty pitcher sitting on a lower shelf of many, many shelves. On each shelf there also sits an empty pitcher. On the very top shelf there is a jug of water. Now tip the jug and pour the water slowly and watch it trickle down as drops and streams of water land in each and every pitcher. Have you guessed what the water is, dear friend? The water is God and begins on the very top shelf. Each shelf is a blip in time, a life, a reality where your spirit stops to ponder. The pitchers are your bodies, or your shells, and it is the water that is the essence of God. Your spirit springs forth from the top where the most Divine begins and trickles down through time expressing and experiencing many dimensions or realities. You call these dimensions lives, but know they all exist at once.

It is possible to traverse time and there have been many that have accomplished this. When you leave this dimension of reality through death, you will of course go with ease and simply pop into somewhere else. It is a very basic matter, actually. Although we do not like to use the word *death*, as it connotes an end to all life, do not be surprised when we tell you that you can easily do that which you think you can only after this so called death takes place. Life does not end. After you cease to exist in this dimension of reality, know that in other places you will ride the cosmic wave. You will remember all that you have experienced as you have bounced through time.

There will be some that will remember clearly, and many that remember without being fully conscious or understanding what is happening. Realities can and will bleed through in various forms, perhaps in a dream, a feeling, a sensation, a familiar face or place, or something vague and not completely known.

What you perceive as mental illness is usually only consciousness that has scattered itself and is not able to focus at any particular place in time. Humans with this affliction have not mastered the art of spiritual discipline. They suck up everything in their astral path without regard or thought as to what it is they do. When landing back in this reality, consciousness sometimes remains scattered in other dimensions and total focus will not be achieved. This is the condition you call mental illness. We tell you that it is not an illness, as you so perceive. The soul sometimes has simply not gained full mastery over dimensional focusing. In many cases, what you view as mental affliction or instability is actually only a manifestation of unclear focus. This sort of focusing is done with intent for the clarification of purpose. In other words, nothing is by accident, but in all things there is purpose.

If there is any confusion at this point, let it be known that there are those who will travel joyfully into other realms without any problems at all. These are the greatly disciplined ones who have indeed mastered all levels of existence. They will always return to that which they reside in and are fully focused and energized at any given point. They are perfectly balanced and will often remember their many soulful journeys into other realms. What one may experience as a dream, the other will know as another time or another place. It will be just as real as this place that you presently dwell in.

We all traverse the Cosmos at varying degrees. Know this to be so, although it is not a matter of jumping in and out of your body. The soul essence streaks across time and expresses at many junctures. What you perceive to be reality now is simply only one of your many places to get off. You have a purpose here, as you have purpose in all realities. Know that your tasks are different, but your purposes are nevertheless the same no matter how many dimensions you reside in. *You* are Light and your soul will streak through time with the precision of a blazing, bright Light. Everyone will know who you are, for you are on a mission of the highest order. Know that you have been given a mission to spark all of Creation with that of the First Light. The First Light is the Great Spirit whose very essence you sprout from. Because you come from this Source of Light, you will be able to do the impossible.

Think of yourself as holding a tall candle and leading the lost through a dark cave. Many will follow because they, in their higher forms, may be able to see that you glow with a certain frequency that others do not possess. Please, at this point we do not wish for you to fall and succumb to an egotistical plane, which exists at the lower levels of human consciousness. We give you this information in order to remind you of that which you already know. We want to jog your memory. Because you exist in this dense Earthly time frame, it is difficult for you to remember. As we remind you of who you are, it is very easy for you to hear our words even though you may not remember who you actually are. Perhaps you are lost and have forgotten why you are here. We come to remind you, but be forewarned that you *will* like what we say concerning your power and purpose. Because you are now in a human form, you will like it so much that it may cause you to be bloated with ego. Ego arises from the lower densities and will destroy not only you, but also others if you are not careful. The spiritual and the ego do not combine well to *Light the way.* Instead of *Lighting the way,* you will *turn them away* because you are operating within a human base instead of a spiritual one. Spiritual things are not composed of ego. Ego is purely a human component. This is important information to you and your mission. Please, take it seriously if you wish to be successful.

It is possible to do work on your planet that you enjoy and which makes you prosperous. Most people are not doing work they enjoy. Life on Planet Earth seems indeed to be sheer drudgery as we watch and ponder your ways. Life only seems to have quality if you make enough money to get the things you need and hopefully the things you want. There are many that are just barely surviving, or surviving with very little. Where is the joy of pure existence? Where is the joy in work? From our perspective, there hardly seems to be any.

You are all trapped in a web of lies and deceit, for you believe that without money all is hopeless. And indeed it is, because you are like a small snowball that rolls and rolls and becomes bigger until finally it is huge. This is how money is. We tell you that you will never make enough and you will never have enough. You will make more, and more, and more, but you will only keep spending more as the snowball grows.

We would like to see another system installed in your world, although we have doubts that it would catch on as what you already have is firmly in place. If changes *were* to occur, it would start very slowly, then as a ripple effect, it would spread out, eventually encompassing all.

As of now, we are concerned about your monetary system as it is breeding a very materialistic worldwide society. Money begets greed and greed begets the materialistic until nothing of any substance is left at all. Glitter and glamour can trap you and trick you into thinking this is all you need. Some of you will forget your true purpose if you allow yourselves to be tricked. This is because it is possible to lose your deepest sense of spirituality, which leads to true purpose when things of the material realm are presented to you. We are not saying these things are wrong, only that your priorities should be in the correct order so that you know the importance of what should come first.

There are many other worlds where the systems you hold so dear are thoroughly unknown. In fact, we tell you the truth when we say that your world system is based largely on lust and greed. Throughout the universe there are places upon places that are far beyond your grasp and they are all based purely on love and trust. Can you imagine such worlds? Yes, it is possible, for we come from such a world and we know of what we speak. A society based on love and trust breeds an entirely different survival system. The basis is not money and what money can buy. The base instead is relationships. In your world it would behoove you to know that connections with other human beings are by far the most important thing. By making connections based on love and harmony, peace is established within a society and people survive by helping people. Your world is not conducive for connecting humans because everyone is too busy and worn out from trying to make enough money.

Societies based on connections instead of money serve a higher purpose for all concerned. Sadly we must say that we do not expect to see any changes in this area. As for now you exist in the lower frequency densities. Although we do not mean to dishearten you, these changes will begin now, but will happen gradually as you ascend to a higher place. The most notable, important and permanent changes, of course, will take place in your very distant future. Our intent is to present and instill these ideas in you now so that that which is very deep in you will become ignited. As you start to consider new and radical ideas you will not only begin the necessary spiritual processes, but you will pass them along and changes will indeed happen one day.

Time is irrelevant. Time is nonexistent. We tell you once again that changes cannot take place completely in this dimension, and now it is our concern that perhaps you will wonder at this remark. Let us clarify further. Important changes are being made by many on a constant basis. You know this to be true, as you have no doubt encountered many belief systems. Belief systems are based in actual spiritual awareness, but remember that because spirituality is something that cannot be seen, it cannot always be gaged properly. See in your mind's eye a very long, winding stairway and imagine the multitude of spiritual levels that exist from the very bottom to the very top. Although each person is standing on a different step, that step is just as important as the one below or above it. At each step, there are a different set of rules, different ways of believing. If you are standing on another step, you may very well feel completely intolerant of another's way of believing and you do not hesitate to tell that person so. What we tell you now is important. Please ponder this carefully. There are indeed people of the Light that are self righteous and judgmental. Instead of leading others to the Light, they may in their zeal be driving them from the Light!

In order to institute changes beginning now, all those of the Light must make a genuine effort to get rid of human ego. Yes, we know this is perhaps a difficult task, especially when you may think we are absurd for even considering that *you* have a problem with ego at all! We say this with a gentle smile as you may be sitting there in a huff with your ego all ruffled. Do not be offended, friend, for we are reminders of all that you already know at your deepest level. Our reminder to you is that you asked us long ago to help you remember and to remind *you* that human ego would most certainly get in the way at the most inappropriate times. We are here now to fulfill the promises that we both agreed to. Although you may think you have no ego to contend with, know that ego is simply part of the human experience. As you are participating as a human, you *will* have ego to contend with.

Time is an illusion, created by the human condition. Time is not linear as you perceive, and so changes cannot happen all at once, but will start from the bottom and work toward the top. It is through those that you perceive outside of your time that will help to affect changes. Outside of yourself, know that you are connected to *others*. These *others* may simply be forms of you that exist in higher places. They come to help just as you go to help in the lower realms. Do not be surprised at this statement, for you also serve a multifaceted purpose.

Know that your dreams are not dreams at all, but places that exist both inside and outside of what you perceive as reality. Last night's dream is just as real as the day you are now participating in. In your dreams, you are many things in many places, not only in this world but also in worlds scattered throughout all of time. You go to others, not only when you are conscious, but at night when you think of yourself as sleeping. Understand that your sleeping time is the most profound and productive time and you are really not sleeping at all! If you wake up tired, it is probably because you have been working very hard. Often, and in most cases, you will not actually remember what it is you did, said or experienced. The human brain mechanism interferes with the soul consciousness, blotting out much of the higher spiritual life that you continue to experience even while you are in human form.

That is why we are here. We come to remind you. Not only do we come to you in book form, but we interact with you in your dreams. Oh, you may not remember us when you awaken, but believe us when we tell you that we are indeed the best of friends. Our purpose is to help keep you on a path of Light. As we instruct you, you will instruct others, not only in this world, but also in your nightly adventures. We say this with a broad grin when we tell you that you do cut through all dimensions with a blaze of Light and glory as you go to those of even lower density frequencies. *You* are of the Light, just as we are. Our job together is to instruct, bring Light and information and shine throughout all of eternity so that Creation will continue to unfold as the Creator intended. As we work in conjunction with you, we remind you again that all creations of Light have a special and divine purpose. We ask that you learn from us and go forth and instruct as to the ways of higher attainment. This is what you were designed to do. We will be with you, and our Creator, the Spirit within, will be with us all.

Maintaining the Illusion

Nothing is by accident. We have said this before. As you may be suffering now, you will suffer again. As you experience joy, you will know joy over and over. Experiences resonate throughout all of time, allowing you to know and experience all that is. You may ask what purpose there is to all of this. We tell you there is none except that which exists to serve you all. Does this sound like a simple answer to a complex question? Yes, it may be, but there is no other way to tell you that all that is, is all that can be. It is nothing more than frequency vibrating to a cosmic tune. Know that this frequency is reduced to minute and invisible particles so small they will never be discovered.

All of reality as you know it is only an illusion. We have said it before and we will say it again. So why it is that we continue to participate in this drama if all is only an illusion? There is no other choice for any of us. It is likened as unto a dream. The dream is you. The dream is us. All of Creation is a manifestation of something beyond ourselves. Think about it. If we are nothing more than a manifestation, then we exist in that which is only an illusion. Would it not be possible to manifest anything at all if everything was only an illusion?

Are you beginning to see, dear friend, what we are getting at? As in a dream, anything at all is possible. So shall you think, so shall it be. It is a simple matter. Speaking of matter, the act of thinking can actually create matter! This is true because thinking is merely an extension of what we perceive to be reality, but know that it is only part of the dream.

Flying is possible. Can you see that now? We tell you that flying is indeed possible, but how many of you will actually be able to do it? As anything is possible, all things have their moment in time. This dimensional time does not recognize flying as possible, therefore, it will be extremely difficult to conjure up the necessary thought enabling you to do it.

Thought patterns group together, creating mass thought. As many of you think, so shall you do. Thought patterns are good and beneficial, yet, they can be dangerous as well. There are groups of people massed together believing in the same things and so those things shall come to pass. We see this demonstrated everywhere, in that there are many kinds of people grouped according to thought patterns and distributed all over the world. Notice the differences within cultural groups or countries. This is why there has always been such turmoil on planet Earth. Frequencies penetrate and express differently throughout the world in the form of cultural clusters.

We would like to point you to Japan for instance as an example of how consciousness is expressed. In this particular country, the mass expression of consciousness is one of collective passivity. Overall, in this society, cohesive and peaceful thought reigns. It connects the people as one. As a result, millions are able to coexist harmoniously without the usual and rampant maiming and killing that happens among other human species on Earth.

Frequencies bombard Earth, which are translated into physical expression in all time zones. Know this to be true, as frequencies are indeed expressed in various forms and translate to that which is physical. Humans are in actuality nothing more than frequency, as all things are.

Based on what we tell you, we hope that you are beginning to see that anything at all is possible. Your life here contains something grand. It is meaningful beyond anything you can imagine. Know, also, that in other places and in other worlds, you continue to exist on higher and yet higher levels.

Religion offers hope, perhaps with a prize or reward in the end. What we come to offer you is total in-Lightenment. Not only will you be *in Light,* but you will also gain new insight as we offer you important new information. The blinders will be removed and you will participate with a new vigor in all that you do. Of course, there will always be those frustrating and dark moments, but overall, as your spiritual comprehension expands and you begin to realize all that you are, your life will continue to grow in richness. You will develop an awareness of so much more as you pull the Light into yourself and continue to question that which surrounds you. As you question and reach for answers, they will be given to you. Sometimes the answers will come to you in the quietness of your soul, or in the heat of the moment, or deep within your heart. Sometimes you will search and ponder and even cry out to a God that seems so far away. Know that nothing goes unheard, but your voice reverberates unto the edges of time, gathering force and coming back to you always. You *will* have your answers. Open a book, listen as someone speaks, turn on the television, contemplate the solitude or the setting sun, There, when you least expect it, will be an answer.

There is nothing we say that has not been said before. We only come as a reminder to tell you what you hear is what you have heard over and over again in many different ways and in many different places. Perhaps in the same lifetime you have even heard the same message. Spiritual matters can be complex. In order to receive the instruction into your human body and mind it is often necessary to repeat over and over again that which you already know in your spirit.

It is imperative that you strive for excellency. We do not mean in the physical realm for that is indeed simple to do. What we speak of is the spiritual realm, for you are far more than what you think you are. You are not a body minus a soul. You are a soul shrouded by a body. You have chosen this body; therefore, it is important to wear it proudly. Although we tell you that the body is truly irrelevant in the spiritual realm of things, it is important in that it is your outer covering.

Concerning the care of the body, it is more a matter of attitude and belief that you are well and happy and healthy. Know that your body is created from your thoughts. As you think you are, so will you be. That is the secret to all things. We stress this again by repeating ourselves. It is important that you begin to realize just how it is that all realities are created from thought. If you believe meat is bad for your body, then so shall it be. If you believe you are growing old, then you will.

It is more difficult to grasp this concept than you may realize. Thoughts have a life of their own and can spring forth, totally out of control, creating worlds that you seem to have no control over. So we tell you that it is easy to *know* that you create your own reality. It is another matter entirely to actually put into practice what you know.

Your thoughts are like your heartbeat or your breath. They *do* have a life of their own. They take you over and often without your conscious consent. Things happen and you have no idea why. We suggest to you that you start listening to your own words. What are you telling yourself over and over? What do you say to others? Listen to your thoughts and know that you are forming your own world. Each of you are a world unto yourselves. Within that world you place things as you perceive them, and please understand that no two worlds are exactly alike. There will be much arguing among you, as you cannot possibly agree all of the time concerning aspects on the spiritual realm. It is difficult enough to agree and come from the same perspective on things of the physical world, so why should there be agreement in the spiritual one?

We want to stress to you the importance of Love. Love is the deciding factor in all things. Know that there is nothing more important. Even to the physical body, Love is like nourishment. Wherever you find Love, you will always find a higher level of attunement. We must tell you that Love comes in varying degrees within each human heart. It is indeed based in the spiritual and not in the physical scheme of things at all. Know that in the same lifetime you will probably fall in Love more than once. Know, also, that there will be times where you experience difficulty separating the purely physical from the spiritual. In human terms, the power of Love is the most wondrous thing to be experienced, but when Love goes wrong it is the worst possible thing.

Understand that feelings and all the accompanying emotions you experience each time you fall in Love are indeed real. They are simply expressed at varying levels. Love is a real emotion. It is the core of your being.

Know that you are Love; therefore, it will behoove you to strive for the expression of this emotion, not only for the sake of your spirit but also for the good of your body. Love not only feeds the soul, but keeps the body healthy and able to thrive. It is here that we must stress that we are not necessarily talking about falling in Love or being in Love, but to simply exist with the spirit of Love contained within you. You are Light and you are Love, both of which are the same.

It is vitally important that you understand and comprehend that there is nothing more detrimental to the human body than anger. Of course, it is always healthy and beneficial to express that which is deepest in you, but anger is created in hostility. Unfortunately, hostility is a basic theme that runs through your time zone. Know that *you,* as a creation of the Light, were not designed to succumb to the negative energy of those that surround you. You must arm yourself and protect yourself because there are those that will try to make you stumble.

Speaking on auras now, we would like to tell you that you have the power to adjust yours. Yes, your aura radiates to that which is inside of you, but know that simply by your thoughts you can indeed change it. We would like to tell you that as you think you are, you will be, thus your aura will change not only according to your emotions and feelings, but also with your wishes and suggestions.

An aura that shimmers as Gold is protective. It is impenetrable. As Light shines Gold, as in the Sun, so shall you shine Gold. Think it and it will be done. While we tell you that a Gold aura will protect you from all spiritual and physical assaults, we also want you to understand that part of the power of a Gold aura lies in the belief that you are indeed strong and invincible. Your belief is what makes it so.

Know that you are not alone, but are connected like a web to many. There is indeed such a thing as Collective Consciousness. We have told you of the Dark Forces and the Light Forces. What we have not told you as of yet, is that you are part of both. There is one ultimate and Prime Creator and all creation originates from there, *both* Light and Dark. You may be feeling a bit confused at this point, as we have told you that you are of the Light. Please understand that Darkness is also of the Light, only with a different face.

We have told you of the Lesser Gods, and yes, they do exist. Creations created under them are indeed of the Darkness. The Lesser Gods were created by the ultimate Creator, but these creations are in a sense lesser than Light.

In essence, all of creation is one and the same, each part, a part of the whole. Know there is order in all things, and all things must have their place. Nothing is random, nothing is by accident and to everything there is a plan. All will work together for good and everything will go on. Ultimately, you may think it will come to an end. Let us pause for a moment to explain. Simply put, there is no end. We stress again that all time exists at the same time. Time is not linear, but more circular perhaps, in that it does not really end at a certain point. It continues around and around and may only appear to end at certain intervals.

Why do we come and tell you of these things? Our mission is one of Love, for we exist on the Love frequency and Love is of the Light. We come to help you evolve, thus evolving ourselves and on and on. Without help from the higher dimensions, creation would indeed remain stagnate at each level. Our hope is to in-Lighten you. In the process, we, as well as many beyond us, will become more in-Lightened. It is then that all of creation will certainly be translated into Light, and only peace, love and harmony will reign supreme.

Chapter Sixteen

Accelerating Love and Awareness

Love is the deciding factor in all things. Know there is nothing more important. Wherever you find Love you will always find a higher level of attunement. Know that Love comes in varying degrees within each human heart. Know also, that in the same lifetime it is more than likely you will fall in Love more than once. Understand that the feelings and emotions you experience each time are indeed real. Love is real. It is simply expressed at varying levels according to human expression.

Speaking of human expression, we must say that Love is certainly displayed at its finest and at its worst in your time zone. What many of you call Love, is not Love at all, or it is Love expressed at a lower level. What each of you are seeking is indeed a longing for the Love you knew before you came to Earth. You have known ultimate Love in the spirit realm. Although you have forgotten, there still remains a vague memory of that which you once knew.

You have, no doubt, also known a higher form of Love in other realities that are levels above your own. You may say to yourself, Love is Love no matter where it is expressed or where it is felt. You have heard the saying that, *God is Love.* Yes, this is true. God is Spirit and Spirit is love in its purest form.

Many of you have a sad place in your hearts as you search for Love on Earth. Spirit creations were meant to find Love and companionship in each other, but it was also meant for you to return to that which you came. If the longing were not there, you would find yourself stuck in one place. Not only would your body deteriorate, but you would never be able to experience the glorious creation which you, yourself, are a part of.

Until your return, Spirit has given you consolation in expressing and feeling Love for one another. This is a great gift, although, many will not truly appreciate that which springs naturally from the heart. It is very important that you know Love is at the center of who you are. Love is at the core of yourself. You must never forget that. If you do, you will find that Love is often difficult to obtain. You seek Love simply because you are Love brought forth in the physical realm.

The Love of two people is indeed a splendid thing. For in true Love, all that you are is allowed to express that which it knows. In loving another, you Love yourself. In caring for another, you care for yourself. Becoming intimate with another, you become intimate with yourself. Knowing Love is knowing yourself...for you *are* Love.

Love is the most important commodity in the universe and beyond. Know that without it, nothing could exist. Love is more important than anything else on Earth, yet you may believe that other things are more important. Without even thinking about it, you may even try to pile up all kinds of things before Love, desperately afraid as you seek to fill up the void. Know that there is nothing else that can fill the void except for Love. You have been created in Love. You need to express it and feel the emotion and be Loved in return.

Why is it that so many repel Love, whether intentionally or subconsciously? There are many reasons for this and some of them are quite complex. Some have been traumatized, whether in this lifetime or another, and may be afraid. Even so, we tell you that it is not always advantageous to stay with the same person throughout an entire lifetime. There will be many that will not like to hear this, but our only motive is to bring you the ultimate truth. Love is more important than anything. If you have not known Love, you have not known true happiness, for happiness is Love. Some believe that happiness is in money or possessions. Know now, that the source of all happiness is in knowing Love, for Love is the essence of all.

Love begins in the spiritual realm. It is powerful and true and pure. There is nothing else and nothing more, other than that of Love. All of you long to know and remember that which you once knew, but your vision has been clouded as you struggle to regain what you recognize as the very center of your being.

Love will often be difficult to find, even though you originated as a spiritual being created in divine Love. You may search, you may wander and even flounder, but your attempts are often in vain as you settle for Love that is only a shadow or hint of the real thing.

Let us repeat what we have just said. It is not always advantageous to stay with the same person throughout an entire lifetime. Please, do not feel dismayed or toss this book aside before we are able to fully explain. Varying degrees of Love can be experienced all within the same lifetime. Some people connect with one person and experience the same degree of Love throughout the relationship with only each other. Others only remain together for fear of moving on or going forward. Changes are very difficult for people, and the anticipated stress that often accompanies these changes may be avoided at all costs.

When two people stay together an entire lifetime, it may be that varying degrees of Love are all being experienced within this one relationship. It is also possible that Love can exist at the same degree within the same relationship over a lifetime, although it is not always at the mutual satisfaction of both parties. More than likely in this kind of relationship, there is acceptance and even tolerance, for various reasons.

We do not mean to condone hopping in and out of Love for the length of time that it takes to move from birth to death. From birth to death is your life on Earth. Your experience of life is what you will make of it. It is not our intent to bring destruction, negativity or untruths. Our only motive is to shed Light on the truth. By doing so, we hope to bring a higher message on the subject of Love.

Considering our vantage point in time, we are able to see what you cannot see. We reside outside of you, yet we are within you, therefore, we are one and the same. By passing information to you from where we are, your evolution will take place faster. We must tell you that we certainly are not the only bearers of truth and knowledge, for there are many indeed. It is here that we must stop to warn you. Not all come with the truth that you need or desire.

We know that if you are reading this material and have arrived at this point, then you are indeed evolving at a rapid pace. Good and evil are all from the same source. If you do not comprehend this, it is now time that you realize how good and evil, and all things above and below and beyond, are various expressions of the ultimate Creator. Although we have talked about the evil forces and the good forces, understand that we all have chosen to express in various forms. It is in those forms that we choose our circumstances. We choose, yet, it is ultimately the choosing by the Spirit that determines where we find ourselves.

We have told you that you create your own reality, and yes, this is true, but at the same time it is Spirit that is creating. That is why it so often seems you have no control over your circumstances. It can feel as if you are adrift upon a wave, riding to where, you know not.

The Spirit is creating as the Spirit chooses to create. Know that you are not a separate entity with a God looking down upon you. You are one and the same, the only difference being that once in physical form, much of the spiritual quality remains at a higher level.

Physical manifestations within physical realms require different frequencies; thus, creativity expressed as physical reality is experienced differently. Know that this is understood by the Spirit, although, you, as a manifestation of the Spirit walk around as if in a fog half the time. Do not be concerned. This is how it should be. If all were experienced on a higher plane, then there would be no need for levels in time. It is through varying levels that *all* forms of expressions can be known.

Back to the subject of Love. Excuse us for the slight moment in departing from so important a subject, but other thoughts intruded. Please know that Love is indeed *extremely* important. Love, in fact, is the prime motivating force for all experience. This is the one absolute, true form of expression, and permeates throughout every level, originating at the top, so to speak. All creations strive for Love. All creations know Love, for they were created in Love. The Spirit *is* Love, and really, nothing more. Not everyone will know or understand this matter, for it often seems elusive. It is not really elusive, but is simply not expressed as it is in the higher realms. Some will give up trying to find it and live their lives alone. Others will die for it, and some will strive over and over to find that which they have known in another time, another place.

Searching for Love is always a good and noble endeavor. Even if you find yourself in and out of many romances or relationships, keep searching, for every time you find Love, you will learn more and possibly know deeper Love. There is nothing on Earth that feels better and more satisfying than the feeling of Love. It is life's elixir. When the heart is broken and Love is withdrawn, nothing feels worse. It is then that you feel poisoned. Know that Love is at the center of your being, although you will indeed feel bad when it is taken away from you by another. Understand that Love can never really be taken from you because you are Love itself. What you feel is only momentarily. In the overall scheme of things, Love will go on and on.

Look at your movies, listen to your songs, read of your history, know of the future. What is the prevailing theme? Is it not Love? Over and over throughout existence, it is Love. You have been Loved, and you will Love repeatedly, not only in this lifetime, but in others as well. You were designed for Love, so it is that we must extol you not to grow bitter and weary, but to remain open for the possibility of feeling so wonderful an emotion. The emotion of Love is the emotion in which you were created!

Love leads us to the topic of sex, for it is in sex that you physically experience the emotion of Love. The emotion of Love is based in spirituality. It is difficult for some to realize that sex has anything to do at all with spirituality. Look at your society for example and all the warnings about sex. This has happened because the spirituality of genuine Love in the context of sex is often missing. Sex is being practiced on a physical basis totally devoid of any spirituality. We are not going to condemn you. Are you surprised? We thought you would be, but that is fine. Once again, we remind you that Spirit will express as it must. If pure physicality is wanted, then that is what will be known and expressed.

We do not mean to add confusion here, but it is always possible to strive for a higher level of awareness. Remember, the Spirit is you and you are the Spirit, and it is within you that all knowledge is contained. Because of the lower frequency that you reside in, it may be more difficult to express on a higher level, although it is possible and many have done so. It is simply a matter of awareness. This is why we come, to bring you information. We are you, and you are us. You might say that we are your higher selves. Together, we are one and the same Spirit, as we are with God.

We have told you that you are special, that you are Light. Know that you are People of the Light because your level of awareness has been greatly increased. You would not be reading this if it were not so. You are capable of so much more than you think. By wanting to be in-Lightened, you will be. As you strive for knowledge beyond your Earthly realm, knowledge will most certainly find you. In ways that you may least expect to increase your spiritual advancement, you will. Not all will be pleasant, but the unpleasant parts will pass and you will find yourself much more in-Lightened. It is here that we must tell you how you may have to endure some suffering for the sake of learning. We like your saying, *without pain, there is no gain,* for this can certainly describe what it may often take to gain understanding and awareness into things that have no rational explanation.

Please, do not be too terribly concerned. It really is not as bad as all that. A spiritual life is by no means an unpleasant experience. It is simply that introspective and sensitive people are often capable of seeing the spiritual meaning and purpose in back of what seems to be going on in the physical world. Unfortunately, such people can easily be hurt, thus, in their deepest pain they reach beyond that which is simply seen with the eyes.

In order to *learn* spirituality, you must become reflective of all and everything around you. A certain sensitivity must be activated to know and get acquainted with your own pain as well as the pain of others. Without sensitivity, true awareness of the human condition is impossible. Not being able to comprehend the pain of others only hardens you to the pain of life. Not only can others suffer around you, but you also, will suffer inside.

There will always be lessons in life. Not so much the lessons that are handed down to you from a judgmental God, but lessons that you will be involved in to further your own awareness. It is through this process that your awareness will accelerate. The harder and more insensitive you

179

are, the harder your lessons will be, for it is there that you learn.

There will be lessons to learn in Love as well. Understand that it is through relationships that you will comprehend Love. It is here that you will grow and develop and remember that from which you came. It is in Love that you can have and be everything, even though you may have nothing else at all.

Perceiving Truth

It is good to gather, absorb, reflect and grow, thus be enthusiastic and ever mindful in your quest for Truth, Knowledge and Light. We have offered you truth, but know that there is so much more than you are able to comprehend at this moment in time. We have given you the truth in bits and pieces, but understand that we expand the information as we go. Do not feel deceived. Know that truth is something which is like a pepple thrown into a pond. It ripples outwardly growing larger and larger until eventually you are able to see clearly the ever widening circles that make up the whole pattern.

You perceive truth according to where you are at. This is why there often seems to be so many different belief systems. Know that what you are doing is actually buying into one of these systems. So, what are we saying and what exactly *is* truth? Let us offer more insight, if you will. It is time now for you to understand that all of what anyone says is true...or some of it is true...or none of it is true. Choose whichever you like. Know that if your frequency is tuned to that truth, then it will be true for you.

Whole groups can find the same purpose and truth at once. They all are vibrating to that frequency. They can make the same thought, or parts of the thought, their reality. There are many that do not understand that ultimate truth is finding out that you yourselves choose your path, your perspective, your circumstances, your lives, your very destiny, as well as your end. And so, whatever you choose to believe becomes your own reality.

Belief systems are important. Without them, life has no texture or spiritual meaning, and life *does* consist of the spiritual. We all originate in a realm outside of the one we think we do. That place is vital to who we are.

What one believes is truth for him, another believes is truth for her. This is why humans squabble and fight such as they do. Each one is consumed and lives completely in their own little universe. We might add that it can get very lonely in there. Humans can suffer greatly from this affliction. Many of you struggle with physical existence, reaching out as you grope for answers, for people, for connections, always trying to comprehend and understand. You may spend much time attempting to find those you feel the same vibration with.

If the many layers of reality could be observed, they would be seen as stacked one on top of another like an eternal pile of pancakes. Think of time as the syrup seeping through and eventually saturating them. Time is not actually as you perceive it, but is only a human made commodity. It is an attempt to organize physical existence into a cohesive pattern so that you may function with some sort of order. It is this order that you have turned into linear time.

The essence of who you are is indeed spirit. The spirit is, for lack of a better word, frequency. We, also, are spirit as all living creations are, yet we exist in another time. Understand, please, that although we exist in another time, we are also a part of you. We are one and the same. There are many of us here and we speak to those of you who are a part of us. That is why you recognize our voice. We are of the Light and we filter down through time to speak to you in this way. You hear us and see us all the time. Understand that a book is not really necessary, although many of you will find that a book is quick and simple. Perhaps you will trust it more. You will not have to try to find the answers in your own mind, but you will see them easily on the pages. You will know in your heart these answers are what you have been longing for. They are your truth.

Your knowledge and awareness have been expanded by now. You have read what we have to tell you. Although you have learned and certainly grown, still, you do not fully comprehend with all your heart and soul. This is natural, because the information we impart to you is certainly of an elevated nature. You must grasp it with a mind that is not totally opened up yet to a higher dimension

Do not hesitate to go back and read and reread as many times as you need to. This is the only way to absorb that which you need in order to expand your awareness and the knowledge of your Light. You will find you must often read things over and over again, that which comes to you from a higher dimension. Do not be disturbed that you cannot remember it all. Know that your spirit is taking it in and is growing and expanding. You are increasing the awareness of yourself as you spread out into eternity. The knowledge that you gain will indeed increase the frequency of the whole. This is what we must all strive for.

Understand that Spirit, or God, if you prefer, does not stand above you on a cloud looking down. No, Spirit does not function as this, nor does Spirit exist in a particular time, but seeps like the syrup into all times, or into all areas of perceived realities. Spirit lives within you and in the very essence of all life. Therefore, know that you are not an individual entity who is separated and stands alone, but that you are one and the same with Spirit.

Perhaps you have been taught that you are indeed a sinful creature who must ask the forgiveness of God before you can be whole again. We tell you that you are already forgiven because there is nothing to forgive. The God you believe in lives inside of you, and is you!

If you feel that you are a separate entity apart from God, know that indeed your existence *is* different because God projects through time into all realities. When you feel the aloneness or the separation, it is because God reaches into the far distant future and expresses there. The lonely disconnected feeling is only that of wanting to reach back into the core of Himself and pulling everything back in. Do not be confused when we use the term "Himself." Words are only human language. There is really no language to express or describe things unseen. With a smile, we tell you that we do our best. At this point, we would also like to tell you we prefer to choose the word *Spirit* rather than God. This is because Spirit best describes something new, whereas you will equate God with all that you have learned previously in your life.

Spirit encompasses all that is. Spirit lives within you and is not outside of yourself. Spirit expresses as male and female. Know that you have been both. Within you lies the secret to all things, for you have been all things and you know all things. You know what it feels to be male and you know what it feels to be female. You know what the trees are. You know what the animals and birds feel, for you have been those things as well. Now it is time to recall and gather into yourself what you know. It is time to exist in that knowing. If you are cruel to an animal, you will know what it feels like to be that animal. There is order to all things and a lesson to be had in the spiritual scheme of things.

You contain the brilliance of a powerful library, which is like a divine hall of knowledge, yet you do not know or understand this yet. You access only minute and limited amounts of information, yet you contain all that Spirit knows, because you *are* Spirit. Why must it be that you do not know all that you are? We have come to help you remember. Understand that in the grand plan, all will take place in due time and when it is suppose to. Realization will increase and awakening will make you blossom like a flower in the springtime.

On human relations, we say to you that most of you will not or have not fully connected to the divine source, so how is it that you can possibly connect to one another at a human level? Divine connection is vital in that this is really the only way you will connect successfully with another. In connecting with Spirit, you connect with yourself, and so it is that you connect with others. We are all linked together only because we exist as one and the same, which all streams forth from the Spirit. You will not be able to connect properly with another outside of the main source, the main source being the original Creator, the Spirit with which you emanate from.

We want to speak to you now of various beings. You are a being. We are beings. We must say there is quite an assortment of beings, not only upon Earth, but spread across every time zone throughout eternity. We call ourselves aliens, but in actuality, you are just as much of an alien to us as we are to you. Alien only means a foreigner in a strange land, and so if used in this way, we are indeed aliens.

In the true sense of all that we are, it is only fair to tell you that aliens are nonexistent, in that you believe time exists in a linear fashion. To explain this further, if time was linear, meaning that if it traveled in a straight line, we would be born in a time zone, then die and return to that which we came. As it is now, we are not born only to die and never return. We are born and we die again and again, and it is happening in rapid succession. Understand that one day, you will be us in the future and we have been you.

It is with this, that we have come like foreigners in a strange land, knowing you, but yet unknown to you. We come in love. We come with a message. We come bringing hope as we show you a way to evolve. It is our desire to help those of you that are willing and ready to be helped. It is our intention to help evolve the human species, for the time is now. Your reality is rapidly accelerating. All that you know will be translated into Light sooner than you think.

Chapter Eighteen

The Process of Evolving

Know that you are indeed connected to all other life sources. You do not stand alone. As you think, so shall another think. As you express, so shall another express. Some of you forget that you are one with all, both good and evil and all things that exist. You strive to be everything that you can possibly be, but know that you *are* what you are suppose to be at this precise moment in your life.

Once more, you do not stand alone. Spirit lives and connects all. It is through physical manifestations as well as things you cannot see, that Spirit expresses. *You* are Spirit. Your neighbor is Spirit. And so the stranger is Spirit also. You are all one and the same.

We have told you that you are People of the Light. And, yes, this is true. You have chosen to express Light, where your neighbor has chosen to express Darkness. It may be that we are an assortment of creations, but ultimately we are connected because we have a common Creator. Remember, even Darkness has been created by the Prime Creator. To every expression, there is a reason and a cause. Nothing is haphazard. Know this to be so.

We want to emphasize the connections of all living things. We want to make it clear that you realize the importance of not only who you are, but who others are as well. We say with a smile, that Spirit does indeed work in mysterious ways. Nothing is by accident and nothing happens randomly. Your lessons are brought to you in many ways. Please, be open to the possibility that another human may be used to bring you information, sometimes in ways you least expect.

You must strive to evolve on a daily and continuous basis. It is through your spiritual advancements that you make contact with the side of yourself that you may know the least about. You cannot learn everything by yourself, but it is through interactions with those around you that you can learn a great deal more.

If you are going through a trying and difficult time with another, know that there is purpose in this. It is through the drama of life that you evolve as a spiritual being. Your Earth time is not only important but is critical to all that you will become.

It is mainly through the many experiences encountered with others that you will develop. Spirit must experience all that is in order to know all there is.

Listen carefully to all that come within your circle. You will most likely not be able to determine the purpose of most interactions. Pay attention. friend, for in doing so you will begin to develop so-called discernment. You will begin to see not with your physical eyes, but with your soul. What you will see with your soul will be very different than that which you see with your eyes. You will open up to receive that which you missed before. In fact, as you open up, you will begin to gain more insight into the true nature and purpose of everything.

In evolving, you will become aware of what you never saw or heard before. Many times, you will indeed find yourself amazed with your interactions. As you evolve you will also attract higher vibes, if you will, and this will serve to contribute even more to your ever-growing awareness.

Know that there are varying levels of awareness. We tell you that it is so much more complex than you could ever realize. Our hope is that you strive to develop awareness of who you really are, for it is that knowledge that will contribute to your evolution. You cannot develop awareness of your spiritual nature by only concentrating on those things in the material realm. Yes, of course, we understand that you have indeed been thrust into such a realm, and, after all, what are you to do? This is the challenge, but know that you chose this challenge above all else.

It is through the often difficult drama of this reality that you will learn. It is through other people that you will grow. It is through all that you feel, experience and know that you will leap ahead. Understand that although you evolve through your physical realm and learn lessons as you could only do on Earth, there is more. Without spiritual insight you will become rather lost, as many are already. Some blunder through this experience called life, and never bother to understand their purpose. They become so engrossed in the physical realm that they forget everything else. They forget that which is most important, for they have forgotten who they are and where they came from.

Others, such as yourself, have reached beyond and caught a glimpse of something familiar. You have never really left behind that which you once knew. You may not fully remember, but you have made an effort to recall the world from which you sprouted. This is as it should be, for it was decided in another place, another time, those of you that would recall and inform others. You, dear friend, are Light. Your mission is to bring the message to others, for they are eagerly waiting.

You will not know who it is that waits. You will not know exactly where to go or what to say. It may even be that you feel inadequate as you speak or inadequate in your actions. As long as you have the desire, the compassion, the sincerity, you will be fine. It is within you as to what you feel for others that determines your actions. If you have evolved enough to be able to see past the body and into the heart and soul, then you will indeed see what others may not.

By having a sincere desire to help others, the correct information will come to you. You will evolve accordingly and you will help others to evolve. As you acquire soul knowledge, your frequency will increase. You will actually spin to a higher tune, if you will, and this will be perceived by others. It is as if you are indeed a lamp and you are being turned on so that your Light glows brighter.

We are informing you of what will happen when you receive information that helps you to evolve. That is our mission. You may have gone through hard times to get where you currently are and do not completely understand all that has happened. We want to assure you that everything is going as planned. You have perhaps been going through a renewal process full of changes and confusion. Whatever the length of time, we know your suffering and turmoil and want to assure you that you will come out of the fire a brand new creation.

Compare the process to a lump of painted clay before and after it has been put in the firing kiln. Before, it was dull and lifeless. Afterwards, it was smooth and shiny and beautiful. This is what you are becoming; a beautiful, bright and shining soul, full of wisdom and knowledge. Do not fret at this point if you feel you are a long way from that person to be. If you have gotten this far with us, then you will indeed become all that you want to become. You are growing now. You are taking into your soul what you need to evolve. It can take many years of Earth life to remember just a part of who you really are. We have come to help you remember. Our hope is to accelerate your knowledge at a much faster rate so that you will become effective that much quicker. It is important, as time as you know it is moving at an alarming rate of speed. There are those that need to transition to other levels now, thus it is vital that there are helpers to guide them through the transition.

You may think it strange that those that are ready to open up to higher levels should automatically have spiritual knowledge at their disposal and be able to help themselves. As we have told you, *all* are one and *all* are connected. If this is true, then it makes sense that every creation is unique. This means there will be a broad spread of attributes. Where one has intellect, another will have practical knowledge and another may express with feelings, and so on and so on. It is as if each creation has come with their own set of gifts. We all help each other. We do not exist in a vacuum unto ourselves.

If you have a longing to know more, then you will. Longings of the heart and soul are always acknowledged. It is in wanting to know your origins that you will find your origins. Look within yourself to know yourself. Reach out to others to help you find answers that you may not find alone. There is always a purpose to every interaction. Nothing is by coincidence. Learning is constantly taking place. Working through so-called Karma is always taking place. You will have dealings here that begin and end in other places. Know this to be true.

Not only will you interact with physical creations, but you will interact on a soul level as well. It is possible to connect to that which you may not think is possible. Look at yourself now. Are you not connecting to what you believe are aliens? Oh, so you may not believe that you, yourself, are connecting, but that you are only reading a book. Dear friend, in reading these pages, you are indeed connecting at a soul level with beings outside of your realm, only you choose to do it through a book. Whether you are reading these words or have written them, know that the interaction is the same. You are learning and growing from the wisdom we have to offer you.

You have gained insight from your meeting with us, have you not? You will see that in time you have indeed evolved as a spiritual being. You can do this through others at all levels. Some, you will perceive and others you may not perceive consciously. It does not matter. You will become that which you were destined to become. It is only important that you continue to reach for the answers. The answers are all around you, but you must be curious in order to receive them. Yes, a curious nature is a wonderful virtue. It will enable you to find things that you never would have otherwise.

Children are curious. That is why they learn so well and acquire so much knowledge in such a short period of time. They clamor to know more and still more. They are constantly reaching out for answers to their questions. We tell you that to be like a child will take you far. You will learn those things that are new and fresh and quite amazing. Children are always amazed, are they not? They are wide open to experience and take in what adults have often set aside. Be like a child and you will learn the answers to many of your questions.

Perhaps you have grown quite bored with the things of your world. Nothing excites you anymore. You require more and more input to get your senses going. It is possible that your senses have become dull because you have ceased to explore. Your senses may be dulled because you blot out that which you should let in. The world may be a boring place because you limit what you allow yourself to see. In other words, you perhaps have narrowed your field of vision until you can no longer see outside the perimeters. In fact, you may be blinding yourself to grand and glorious things which lie directly outside the perimeters of your narrow field. We implore you to open your eyes wide and strain to take in the larger view. It may be a shock at first, but after a while you will grow accustom to the greater detail and will even want to add more details.

There is so much more beyond your scope of vision. To break past the barriers you must allow yourself to open up. Only then will you begin to yearn for more. We cannot tell you everything, but you must find out for yourself. We have told you so much already, but it is *you* that must make the discoveries. It is in *your* own heart that the truth shall reign supreme. We are here to help you evolve, but at the same time we certainly do not want to start another religion! It is so easy to start religions in your world. A bit of truth here, a bit of truth there, and before you know it a religion is born. We tell you that religions have even been founded on creatures from other worlds that have entered into your realm. And the truth is, many of your great and wondrous holy people were from other worlds, other times and other places. We all help to help each other. Know this to be true.

You never know when someone you meet may be that someone you need. Stay alert for information and you will be pleasantly surprised. If you want to evolve, then there will be those that will come to you. They may not be what or whom you expect, but that which you least expect. Attune yourself to receive information at a higher level and you will. If you expect the worst, then that is what you will encounter. You will not receive those things of a higher spiritual nature, but will attract the lower elements. Know that this involves inanimate objects as well as people, creatures, creations and situations. It involves *all* things. You can draw to you those that will help you or denounce you. The choice is yours. You draw those not only of this realm, but of other realms as well. That is how we are here. You have drawn us with your intention to be helped, and we have heard and we have come.

It is as if you have spent a lifetime waking from a deep sleep. You perhaps look back on what you have done and you wonder in puzzlement that you could do what you have done at all. There has been joy, there has been pain, but most of all there has been a process that you have probably not fully realized. You have spent a lifetime evolving and here it is that you have arrived. So, what do you make of yourself? Have you made progress? We do not mean progress on a physical, material level, but on a spiritual level.

It is not always easy to ponder on the spiritual progress of one's soul. It takes many years and many tears of toiling to develop spiritual insight. Sometimes it is only through hindsight that you can see that you have made any progress at all. Meditation and reflection are valuable tools in that they are a form of self-analysis. Look deeply inside your self and you will begin to put the pieces together. Pay attention to your dreams as well, for they are not as insignificant as you may think. Analyze not only your waking time, but your sleeping time as well. For we tell you that as you dream, you also learn, for it is in your dreams that your soul experiences all its shapes and forms.

Developing Your Soul

It is through your spirit that you are free. It is through your heart that you feel. Through your body you are connected to your world, and it is your body that you will leave behind. Know that your spirit soars free at the moment of death. Many of you grieve over this process only because you lack understanding of the process of leaving the earth realm. How is it that you have forgotten that from which you came? We come to remind you by putting a spark of remembrance in you. When you hear our words, you will come to know that which you have forgotten and you will begin to awaken.

You long to know what you have forgotten. That is why the human condition is often so sad. On the surface of humanity, all can appear well, but dig below and the sadness lingers deep where no one sees. We know this to be so, for we can see where you cannot. We have also been where you are and have evolved to a higher point, just as you will.

The sadness comes from losing a connection to that which you once knew. You try to find it in all sorts of places, but often what you try to find is elusive. The search goes on, day in and day out as you struggle to maintain and find happiness. Can happiness be found at the Earth level? Yes, we assure you that it does exist, but is not necessarily to be found in things of the physical realm. Perhaps, for fleeting moments, happiness prevails, but with true happiness there is contentment and peace that can only come from within.

What do we mean by within? It is within, at the very core of yourself that your spirit resides. That which you are on the inside is not what you are on the outside. Your body is simply a shell that houses what activates you. Observe a dead human and you will immediately understand that all life is certainly gone. The facial features, the body itself, has gone flat and lifeless, sometimes so much so that what you once knew is hardly recognizable. We are sorry if you think us morbid. A body is a body, and the important substance is what occupies the body. Understand that we are trying to make a point and come from another perspective entirely. Bear with us, please, as we do try mightily to be sensitive.

We do not want to instigate worry, fear, or concern. Our motive, always, is to bring information in the most pleasant and positive way possible. Creation is so very complex and there are always those things which can be extremely delicate to convey. We are so excited to have reached you at last and to bring all those things that will help you to evolve. Please, realize there are many of us here that have learned how to reach you. At this time, there are not as many of you that are willing to connect and tune into us, although the numbers *are* increasing.

We are as many and varied as you. We may come to you individually or as a group or a unit. We may bring different information. Some of us, just as you, are more interested in conveying history. Some of us are more blunt and want to tell you everything - the good, the bad, the beautiful and even the ugly parts. Some of us have more knowledge or wisdom than others. Some are more practical, sensitive or even romantic and wish to talk about love and such things.

It is our hope and intention to bring you only the best. We want you to grow and evolve. We want you to know as much as possible. We do not believe it is to your advantage to fill you with fear. There are indeed fearful things in our creation, but our focus at this point is to now bring you knowledge that there is a higher way if you look within yourself. You contain everything you need to know. By tuning into your higher self, you *will* evolve.

Perhaps your question might be, what is my higher self or *where* is it? As we have said, creation is complex. Trust us, please, when we say to you that your higher self not only dwells within you, but can reach you from other dimensions. It is often extremely difficult to get in touch with your complete self from where you dwell at the Earth level. You spread through time, like a ray from the sun. It is here, at our point in time that you stretch and reach for, as we reach back through time to you. Know that you are us and we are you. We are you at a higher more evolved place. It does not stop here, but continues through eternity.

Know, also, that you contain layers that translate into multitudes. You are not simply a mere Earth creature standing alone. If you were to arrange mirrors at certain angles, you would observe hundreds of replicas of yourself. This is how creation is. You extend far beyond what you think you are. How you evolve here will affect how you evolve in other places. You are composed of many components, and it is those components that form your spiritual foundation or basis.

The important components are made from spirit and not from flesh. The components of flesh will not survive from one realm to the next, but will turn back into the elements from which they came. It is only your spiritual components that survive and go on. These are the vital parts that make you what you are. If you focus purely on the physical, then you will surely wither and your spirit as a whole will suffer. It is to your benefit to develop and evolve yourself. We are your future selves. We have the ability to come and help show you the way. By learning those things they do not teach you in school, you are learning the real essence of life. By learning to navigate the invisible world, you learn how to deal with the physical world.

It is not by dealing with the world on a physical basis that you learn how to navigate the world. It takes much more in order to survive. It involves senses beyond the usual physical senses. You are so largely underdeveloped that you do not realize at this point just how much you are lacking. This is why you stumble and fall and get knocked down so much by life. You are equipped, but your equipment sits on a shelf unused.

You need spiritual training. You need wisdom that is not of your world. This wisdom can only come from higher sources. Do not be afraid to tap into these higher sources for they will serve you well in your own survival on a physical level. Learn to see what is past seeing with the eyes. Learn to hear more than what your ears can hear. Learn to feel more than you can feel with your fingers. Learn to taste that which is tastier.

You can evolve past the usual ordinary senses by focusing on that which you ordinarily do not pay much attention to. Find a quiet spot and reflect on a bird in the sky as it catches the currents in the air, dipping and diving. Even the act of feeding bread to a flock of birds can be a way to a peaceful interlude. There can be joy and fascination in watching the interaction of the birds as they struggle and fight for every crumb. In watching them, you watch yourself.

We are reminding you of the simple things in your world. We call them simple, yet they are far more complex than you realize. Your eyes have been trained to see things in a certain way. You have grown numb to what is beneath the surface. You have closed off your senses to that which is important. It is seemingly in the simple things of your reality where most things can be learned. By reflecting on those things, you will pierce through a veil and began to see more and more.

Look at a flower or a blade of grass and wonder at the awe of it. Stand at the shoreline of the ocean and contemplate the scene with the senses of your soul. Think on the composition of the water and how it moves. Think on these things and realize that there is much more in back of what you see.

Your world is a painting in motion. It is simply molecules at the physical level that are gathered at varying frequencies, yet, it is you that holds the illusion. Know that it is you that makes the waves crash against the rocks and the clouds gather in the sky. All is connected and created by Spirit. *You* are Spirit. What you see is what you have created at the highest level of yourself. God is at the top rung of the ladder, so to speak, and you are the lower rungs, as we certainly are as well.

You might say that we come in the name of God. We come to declare that God lives inside of you, as Spirit does indeed dwell inside of us and inside of all creation. You are God and we are God. Throughout the ages of life on Earth, information has come in various forms. The world was given certain information when Jesus came. We tell you now, this man was not who you might think he was. He said, "My ways are higher than your ways. My world is higher than your world. Where I come from, you cannot go." Does this help you to see that he was not an ordinary human from planet Earth?

Jesus, and the others that have come, have not always been understood, especially by the ancient or older civilizations that existed at that time. These special and in-Lightened ones have been perceived as gods. Know that much of your history, when it speaks of gods or God has grown out of misunderstandings and lack of comprehension.

The stories and pictures are there, but you choose to ignore them. This was because the comprehension at the Earth level was at a simple state, a more primitive level, if you will. The stories have grown and evolved, encompassing the world as religions. It is now time to take a closer look. You, of the Light, are existing at a much higher level and are now able to comprehend what was not understood before. You know now, that we are not gods and that we have not come to bring another religion. Our only purpose is to bring information that will help you to evolve.

You can evolve by taking in information that you need to develop your soul. Soul information is different in that it aids your spiritual development. We are not saying that all things that you experience are not beneficial to your development. Certainly *all* things aid you in your progression, even those things that seem to be of an earthly nature. The difference is that soul information is given to you, or comes to you at a certain level. You perceive it to be of a spiritual nature. You take it in, knowing consciously that it is different than your usual learning lessons of life.

If you are consciously and spiritually evolving, you will be fully aware of it, although you are always evolving at all levels. What we are saying here is that there will be those that choose to ignore that from which they came. The Earth realm has completely captured them. Know that you are here, that you are Light and you are certainly participating in much more than an Earth realm level. If you have come this far with us, you are certainly seeking to evolve spiritually on a conscious level. You are not flailing through life, learning your lessons haphazardly, but are diligently striving to remember all that you really are. In the process of evolving, you have begun to realize that you are simply more than a body. You are becoming aware of why things happen to you. You may not be fully cognizant of everything, but you are beginning to see there is an invisible world in back of the physical one that you see with your eyes.

This invisible world that we speak of is the spiritual world in which you first sprouted. We use the names with which you are familiar with. Invisible and spiritual. These are simply human words to describe that which is *not* describable. Simply know and understand that you have not sprouted first in the physical world, but came forth from another realm. You are spirit first. Then you manifest in a realm that appears as physical.

This physical realm has characteristics unlike those in the spiritual realm. You might say that existence or survival is a bit more intense, not only in a physical sense, but emotionally as well. You feel things like you would not feel them at the higher realms. Putting the spirit, so to speak, in a body is not the easiest of things to accomplish! It can be quite a chore sometimes to carry on, such as you do, and to refrain from completely breaking down in all the many situations that you encounter in your time upon Earth. We tell you this, knowing full well, that although you may have many despairing moments, you have come here with a plan. It can often be difficult, but all that you do, and all that you encounter are exactly those things that will take you to where you need to go.

You *will* survive! You were designed to survive. You have a purpose and you will fulfill that purpose. It may be that you have known in the deepest part of yourself that there was something that you were suppose to be doing. Perhaps it is so that you even have a mission. You may not know what it is now, but you feel the stirrings. It *will* be revealed in time. Be patient, dear one, for if the time is not now, then it will be at a time when you are fully prepared and ready to pursue that which you were brought here for.

You may have many moments of sadness. This is okay, for in your sadness, you feel the moods and movements of spirit. Spirit is emotion. By experiencing and expressing your emotion, you come alive and feel the Spirit part of yourself. When you feel joy, you feel Spirit. When you feel sorrow, you feel Spirit; even in your anger, you are feeling that which you are made of. It is when you feel nothing that you have shut yourself off to

209

what you are. It is important that you strive for feeling. Of course, we do not want to condone emotions that run amuck! We always think it is beneficial to have some measure of discipline and control. We might even say that it is absolutely vital and to your benefit that you learn to control and even corral your emotions. This is necessary, in that human emotion can spring forth, creating a life of its own, and even running rampant. This is true of your current level of reality.

Spirit is feeling, but feeling can be big, and warm, and generous. It is our hope, that as you evolve, your emotion will be honed as unto a higher level. Higher level emotion is calmer. It is the feeling and passion without the parts that cause trouble. Strife and turmoil are always of a lower nature. Know that when these kinds of situations or interactions occur, you are operating from the lower levels.

We know and understand that you often yearn to be the best that you can be. It may be that you are at a transition point in your life. You know in your heart what it is that you must do and be, but still, you continue to find yourself with troubles. Please, do not despair. Understand that the longing and desire within you is what is important. It will be just the thing that helps to propel you up the spiritual ladder. It is in your turmoil where you battle the forces, and little by little, you move toward a higher place.

It is in those places of turmoil where you will not always consciously recognize that you are evolving. You will fall and agonize and despair, but you will learn and grow, and reach places that are important in your development. Soul knowledge will come to you. You will absorb it, such as you absorb earthly knowledge by listening to an instructor in a classroom, reading a textbook, or studying for an exam. You are reading these words, and it is a simple matter that you will absorb into your soul that which you read. You *will* evolve and awaken to the truth of who you are.

Soul knowledge will come to you in many forms, by reading, by listening, by studying, and through the hard lessons of life. You will be done here one day and then you will move on. You will not simply end here, but you will indeed continue your journey. Understand for now that you have gotten off here, but only for a very small moment in time.

Chapter Twenty

Basic Spiritual Concepts

You are so enthusiastic in your quest for truth, knowledge and Light. This is good. It is good to gather, absorb, reflect and grow, but often times during this process you may start to feel confused. We smile when we tell you that just about everyone that offers you truth can sound wonderful and even glorious. We tell you that there are indeed many ways and many truths. So which way is right and which truth is the ultimate truth? Every religion, every channeler and every psychic have their own handle on truth. There can often seem to be many similarities.

Truth? What is it and who really has it? We tell you there is no one truth. Please, do not be dismayed. Just as you may have thought you found truth, we tell you there is more than one truth. The dilemma is that creation is far more complex than you can imagine. A simple thought such as *truth* goes far beyond what you know. It will take you deep into other places and other realities.

There are many so called levels. All of creation exists at different levels and is constantly fluctuating. At any one point it is possible and more than likely that you will perceive according to where you are at that particular moment in time. This is why there are so many different belief systems. We have told you this before, but we want to remind you again.

There are certain basics to be aware of. First and foremost, you are spirit. It is only after this that you manifest as something physical. We are not going to tell you that you necessarily become a human form when manifesting in the physical, simply because that would not be correct. Spirit comes first. It then gathers and manifests into the physical realm. The physical realm appears in many places in the universe. It is simply frequency that has been stepped down. Know that spirit manifests in many forms on Earth. As we have said, this does not always mean in human form. This is simply basic, to know that frequencies are tuned at various vibrations and create a multitude of assorted manifestations.

You are evolving. You have certainly realized at this point in your life that you are more than what you see. This is another basic concept that many have not grasped yet. The human form is simply that which houses the most important ingredient of who you are. Like a shellfish, your body is your shell. The essence that lives inside the shell is your soul. Believe it or not, there are many humans that never consider much beyond their physical form. For you, this is basic knowledge and it gives you wisdom. As you have gained in your learning that which is important to know, it is now vital that you take it to others. Please, without arrogance, remind people that they *do* indeed contain a soul!

Not only must you remind those that have forgotten, but you must know and understand the true power of who *you* are. There are those that do not know the power that is contained within their bodies. The spirit is powerful and can do all things! It is through your spirit that you know all things. It is through your spirit that you truly operate as a being. Most beings on Earth only operate partially. Instead of whole beings, what we are seeing are half beings or even less than half.

Realizing your own power is certainly a basic concept to understand. Many residing on Earth believe that true power dwells not within, but outside of themselves. In believing this, they are seriously limiting all that they can be. If you wait for a power beyond to put things into action, then there may be no action or there may be wrong action. You are the one that contains the power. It is *you* that can control the circumstances and events of your life. Often it seems that life controls you. You flounder and flail and look beyond yourself to a God for help. Know that you are God! You are God at your highest level.

If you have the power, then why do things seem to run amuck so much of the time? It is here that we bring up the subject of karma, as you may have thought of that yourself. As we have said before, creation is indeed complex. You understand only in the smallest way what this word *karma* means. Your karma word encompasses so much more than you can imagine. You apply this concept in most cases to a very narrow and limited view of things, as it is difficult to see the whole. You may think you see, but your perception does not always include all aspects of creation.

You are much bigger and more powerful that you know. You are Spirit. Your spirit is not small, nor is it simply encased in one body in this time and reality. We have told you that your spirit goes on and on into endless eternity. Please, listen carefully here. You act and react to all things in all times and places. You must look beyond your experiences here and realize that what you do may affect yourself in other realms. You exist here, you exist in the past and you exist in the future. There is no such thing as past lives. Know that you experience yourself at all levels and in all places. It is happening now, not in the past. What you do anywhere else in time affects yourself at this moment in time.

You exist in the future and even beyond the future. You exist at the level where you are God. We are going beyond simple and basic concepts at this point. What we tell you can often be difficult to bring into language. Precise and accurate words do not exist, even to describe much of what we have to tell you. It takes many words, linked together to form patterns, images and ideas. In the higher realms, information and knowledge is not gained through the reading of words. It is absorbed through the spirit, so to speak. We do our best to give you a clear and accurate picture. Still, our words are only words. Hopefully, they will serve the purpose of presenting information to you. It is our hope that they will jog your spirit memory. We can tell you many things, but it is you that will put the pieces together and begin to remember.

You remember in fragments. Over a lifetime, you have remembered in bits and pieces. The portion of the whole is still largely unencountered. You will not fully remember or realize all of that which you are in one lifetime upon Earth. It will take many lifetimes in many places to even begin to come close to knowing who you really are. Imagine that your spirit travels a wave in time.

The wave can throw you into the air as you topple and thrash upon the choppy waters. You swim for your life and you learn. It can be both exhilarating, and yet, you can suffer. These are the lessons that you must go through.

Lessons. We do not mean to give this word a bad feeling. If we knew of another better word, we would certainly use it. Much too often, the word *lessons* denotes a negative feeling. This is because of your school system. School in many places on Earth is not exactly a good experience. In fact, as long as we are here we might take this opportunity to give you our feelings about your school system. And yes, we *do* have feelings. We are not the kind of beings you depict in your TV shows such as the emotionally devoid Dr. Spock!

Where were we? Let us get back to the subject at hand. School. If you have bad feelings about the word *lessons*, it is because of your experience with your schooling system. You force your children out of your homes into a situation where you no longer have any control. From the time they are very young, you have no idea who is imprinting them or what is going on. Know that many of your teachers may put information in your children's heads that you may not agree with at all. Not only that, but you do not know what else goes on or takes place. Children grow up, and the damage shows up. Many adults are damaged or traumatized because of the subtle forms of manipulation, control and humiliation exerted upon them by these so-called teachers or adults in charge.

We see that your rights as humans have been completely taken from you. We see that your children are taken away, and in allowing this to happen, you as a civilization will suffer. Please, understand that you cannot mass bunches of young souls together without the proper love and care. Not only this, but the *lessons* imparted to your young ones may be the wrong lessons. Your children are not only imprinted by other adults, but they can also suffer tremendously at the hands of their peers.

You may wonder why we are talking about your educational system now. This is certainly not spiritual, or is it? As a solid and physical civilization, you must learn things of a physical nature as well. It disturbs us to see the young ones massed together like they are on planet Earth. The lessons that are learned only make to harden each individual that has gone through this abhorrent system. Even though you may be much older and wiser now, do you still not suffer from experiences encountered while forced into this mass educational system? Have these lessons not become a part of who you now? You are what you are partly because of what you have gone through in this one lifetime.

Look at yourself. Are you successful in the work that you do? Do you not appear to the outside world that you are in control? Certainly you look strong enough. You act strong enough. But, why is it that you have anger? Think about this for a moment. Was it at an early age that you were forcibly torn from your mother and thrown into a situation that was totally bewildering? You were a new soul upon this planet Earth, and yet, they would not allow you to be nurtured and educated in the safety net of your family.

This way of schooling is a fairly recent method of educating your children. At one time, and still in some places on Earth, children learn in a completely different environment than one of a bewildering mass of young souls thrown together. This way is detrimental to the very life forces upon your planet. You cannot toss your children out into the world and expect your civilization to stay whole.

You can begin to see the signs of decay and crumbling. New souls upon entering life on Earth need to be sheltered for a length of time before they are released to outside forces. The time has come now, where even newborn babies are being turned over to others. They are put into these mass group situations where only harm can come. There is certainly not the proper nurturing, love and care that they need. These babies are growing up in a group of unrelated beings. Do you really know what goes on with your baby? What about the other children? What about the adult in charge that is trying to take care of all of these children? Is it for love or for money that they do this work?

Why are you tossing your children away? The lessons they learn will only harm them. These kind of lessons will only serve to make them mean and angry and alienated. Look at your own anger, sadness, aloneness, or even your rebellion. Somewhere in time, what was done unto you has now become you. If you came from a loving family, then why do you suffer so? Do your sufferings come from what you experienced as a little one at the hands of your peers or adults in charge?

You may wonder why we have become so passionate about this subject. It was the word *lesson* that prompted us. We found it impossible to make an analogy of the lessons you learn in the spiritual realm and the lessons you learn in your educational system. The educational system in much of the world is leading to the destruction of society. From our vantage point, we can see that clearly.

Know there are worlds where tender loving care is bestowed upon the young ones. This means there are systems in place that nurture the development of not only body and minds, but hearts and souls as well. It is recognized that in order to produce a highly productive and evolved species, much thought and detail must go into what becomes of the young ones. Yes, you might produce a highly technical society, but in the meantime, it will most certainly become soulless.

Chapter Twenty-One

An Awakening Within

We will cover all topics, if not here, then in other places. We are beings in another time. Although we may be your higher selves, we are not divine. Even God, which is your very highest self, is not divine in the sense of the word. Speaking of *words*, we can find them terribly limiting. If we could apply our *own* words, things would go much better, if only you knew our language. We will not go into the details of our language, as it really serves no purpose at this point. Simply know that we can speak any language, but that our language gives a more expanded and detailed view in much less words, or with no words at all!

It is here where we want to tell you that we have clearly seen the human condition. We have been observing for a long time. We are saddened by what we see and it is our utmost desire to want to help. There are many that are afraid for outside sources to come in and help. There are many that live on a simple level. They refuse to look beyond to what is or what could be. We would like to bring methods and ideas that will help. We realize that most of humanity will not be reading helpful hints from the Pleiadians, so it is up to you to take what you have learned and spread it around. You can do this, not necessarily by stating that you got your information from higher sources, but simply in your own gentle discussion or remarks with others. During conversation, or when certain topics come up, you will have the resources within because you have evolved. You have most certainly begun to realize by now all the possibilities and are awakening to the divine nature of who you are. By your conversation and contact with others, they also, will begin to awaken as if from a dark and deep slumber.

We have talked about the suffering of Earth's people. Much of what you have gone through as a young one has led to your current suffering. We would like to tell you that there is a way to console and help that, which you have been. Not only can you reach back into the past, but you can also reach forward into the future. We are your future and we are reaching back to help you, are we not?

It is possible to reach back into time and help yourself. Go back to an early point, perhaps a place where you believe there was some kind of hurt or injustice done to you. Please, know that you will not remember all those places where you encountered suffering. In fact, it is most likely that you will not remember most of what has happened to you. For now, simply pick a point where you do remember. Who or what was it that hurt you? What feelings do you have inside of you? How has this incident affected you in your current life? Has your behavior been altered by it? Stop reading and close your eyes if you need to think about this for a moment. Then come back and read on.

If you have anger inside of you, there is a reason why. Not all behavior is brought in with you at the moment of birth from other lives. Much that shapes and forms you, and even deeply affects you, is because of what you have encountered in the Earthly realm. Go back to yourself at a younger time. Look at what you see. Is it hazy or is it clear? Sometimes you may not remember the incident, the actions or the words spoken, but you remember the feelings. You still have those feelings encased in your heart. If you were to tell someone of this incident, no doubt, you would still have the feelings even though a number of years have passed.

You are still feeling the pain. You still hold onto it and have allowed it to influence you, and build and shape you. If you lash out at people in anger, are you simply reacting to the hurt that people instilled in you a long time ago? If you cannot trust love, is it because what you thought was love turned into something bad? Have you put a wall around yourself to protect you from others because you have been so hurt by them? Have you severed the connections in some way or form that will not allow you to feel the pain of others? Has your heart been cast in stone, never to hurt again because you, yourself have been so severely hurt?

Once again, we tell you there is no psychiatrist, counselor or religious leader on Earth that can help you like you can help yourself. It is really so simply that we are quite amazed that most of humanity does not understand how to do this. It has only been this way because of lack of information and understanding. It is the belief in a God that lives outside of yourself and who you think controls you. It is a belief in religious books that limit your understanding to know your own true power. Simply stated, it is a lack of understanding of who you really are and what you can really do.

Reach back in time, as we are now reaching back in time to you. Reach back in time to your suffering self. See that person clearly. Know that it is you that is still suffering. That person continues to exist and to experience the pain. You can help right this moment. Reach back. Go to that hurting child or that hurting adult. Go to wherever you must go, but go. Speak to yourself at that point in time. You do not have to speak out loud. Thoughts will transmit to that time. Visualize yourself consoling, hugging, patting and offering love and understanding. You can even try these methods of care and apply them to yourself here. You may be surprised with how patting your face can make you feel, as you verbally console yourself. As we come to you with words of wisdom and guidance, you can do the same for your past selves.

You have learned a lot in your Earthly journey. From this point in time, know now, that you can indeed go to your other parts and help there, just as we come from the future to help you here. By reaching into the past, you can heal many aspects of your soul. Your soul will become awakened at all points, and will manage better the pain and injustices of expressing in those denser physical realities. We would suggest to you, that you frequently and daily remember to send Light to all parts of yourself, thus acknowledging that what you are now is only a small part of the whole.

We come as soul healers. We come as helpers. We bring information that will help you to evolve. Our intent is one of highest purpose and honor. We honor that which you are. We honor all beings that enter into the Earth frequency. To live a life upon planet Earth is one of the highest honors.

We must tell you that it is not an easy place to live! The frequency is dense. This makes for an often difficult journey on many paths. You must step down your energy in order to experience life on Earth. This is not an easy chore, but one of intense decision made by each of you that has come to reside here. We admire your courage!

The challenges you must face will require you to learn of power. We have talked about this before, but we must remind you again. Reading about power is one thing, but becoming power is another. You may read of these things first, or rather, we might say that you are reminded as you read. You will begin to awaken deep within. You will remember and know those things which are truth for you. You will begin to know what is in your heart, and you will attempt to follow where it leads. Understand, that it is within your heart that you must go, for this is where you will find your true answers. Of course, we speak of your heart, but know that heart is spirit. It is by your spirit that you will be lead. It is your spirit that guides you always. Spirit can come to you in a higher form, just as we have come to you, or God can come to you. Know that we are all one and the same.

We come only as a reminder, as you, yourself, are reminded. We do not come as a religion. Be careful that you do not create another religion from that which we teach. It is so easy for beings upon

Earth to do this. Residing in the lower densities that you do, it is often very easy to look beyond yourself and assign glorious importance to that which seems above you. It is easy to make gods of those that come to in-Lighten. It has been done often throughout the ages of time. Those that have come in physical form have been glorified and made into gods. Those that have brought messages of in-Lightenment have been turned into gods or into holy people. This was truer in ancient times, although there will be those in more recent times that will be revered in the future. Remember though, we have told you that all time exists at the same time. When we speak of past, present or future, we simply use this as a marker or reference for certain periods of time.

Truly understanding the concept of time will help you to help all parts of your soul. In understanding how you do not simply exist in one time zone, you will begin to understand how all of creation works. You are composed of all parts of creation. Your spirit continues like a circle and experiences all things. It is never ending. It dabbles in time picking up bits and pieces and adding unto itself. Your goal is to increase the awareness of your entire spirit. You can, in no way, fully function as a whole and complete unit without knowledge of the other parts.

Understand that there will be those forces designed to keep you from knowing. Your job will be to increase the Light of yourself. The trick in doing this is in the gathering of knowledge and wisdom. We give you not only soul knowledge, but knowledge that will help you to navigate your world. In learning to navigate your world, you will begin to learn about yourself. In learning about yourself, you will increase your awareness.

The knowledge of your world is certainly different than the knowledge you will gather in the spirit realm. Both forms of knowledge are necessary. In learning to function as a physical being upon Earth, you must begin to decipher hidden codes that you are not consciously aware of. Hidden codes are hidden from you because you are not fully functioning as a complete unit. We tell you that you will never completely and fully function with all of your senses in your worldly realm. We tell you, that we also do not function completely as whole beings even where we are at. We inform you of this only so that you do not make us into the gods that we certainly are not.

It is always at each juncture in time that information needs to be learned and processed. There are always dimensional crossovers in helping to disseminate this important information. Not only is the spiritual information given, but quite often information is given that helps to accelerate the life and existence of that plane. This kind of information involves those things that must take place on that particular physical level. Yes, what we are saying is that beings upon planet Earth have certainly tuned into higher levels to bring what you now may take for granted. We speak of such things as your electricity, technology, medicine, art or music. Great inventors have often tuned to other dimensions and have brought forth many wondrous things.

How is it that you are now able to see within the dark spaces of your home? Light has been made manifest as a physical property. The ability to receive such information as to the invention of physical light is directly attributed to the mechanism of the inventor's mind. The mind in all such cases of wondrous inventions has not remained stagnant, but has traversed the levels of time. Information can be plucked from other places and brought forth in any dimension.

It is here that we give you information from another dimension. We give you knowledge and wisdom that will help to awaken your soul. Know that it is always up to you as to whether you will receive that which is given to you. Receiving soul knowledge is often based on the level of learning that you are at. Your willingness is also often a great factor as well. You must often strive to receive that which is sometimes difficult to comprehend or undersand. It can certainly be an exercise of the mind to open up to knowledge outside of the earthly realm. The physical realm has a way of trapping you into its illusions.

When your soul arrived on Earth in the form of a newborn baby, your perceptions were not as they are now. You had not yet completed the transition from the spiritual to the physical realm. Look into the eyes of a newborn and you can plainly see that the spirit comes and goes. It is indeed a slow awakening to the Earth plane. This is why babies sleep so much of the time! Their souls are still traversing the spiritual realms. In other words, they are gone much of the time, their souls blipping in and out of different dimensions.

The physical aspects of the Earth realm are indeed a tremendous effort as you come forth from your mother's womb. It is a jolt or a shock for the spirit to fully and suddenly experience such density. It does take some getting use to, thus, the blipping of the soul in and out of many dimensions. The soul must gradually adapt and adjust to that which it is not quite use to doing. Know that every being born upon Earth has its own time and rhythm. Some adjust quickly, and some never quite do. In most cases it takes a lifetime, but still, the struggle is always there. You are spirit first and the physical manifestation is created afterwards. Even in your bodies, you never completely forget that which you come from, although you do forget easily, otherwise, the longing to return to your spirit world might indeed overwhelm you. In a way it is all designed so that you forget.

You will spend a lifetime learning, evolving and awakening. You will suffer, you will feel pain and experience joy. Your span of time in the Earth realm is only for a fleeting moment. Yet, as you experience it moment by moment, it will often seem to be an eternity. You will run through parts of your life with hardly a moment of rest. Other times, all you will want is rest. The years will roll by, one by one, slowly at first, until they seem to speed up and finally to accelerate so quickly that you will be amazed and wonder where time has gone.

This is the nature of time. Your time will begin to close in on you until there is no time. Your body will begin to wear out despite what you do. Know that the body and spirit are synchronized and they work in harmony until your end of time on Earth. You will have learned and experienced all that you need, until one day it will be time to move on. You will blip away from the reality of Earth time and focus elsewhere, and that will become your new time. Although you reside in all places at once, what you perceive now is what you know.

With what you now know and have learned up to this point in your life, it is our hope that you have accelerated your spiritual evolution. It is our intent and purpose to cause an awakening within the deepest parts of yourself. Although we have brought you information, understand that it is *you* that has attracted a higher energy source to yourself. It is *you* that has sought after what we have given you. It is *you* that will continue to seek that which you need, here and now, and forever more.

An
*U*ncommon
Index

Index

Index

Index

Index

cultural clusters 162
culture 116
current level of reality 210

D

dabbles in time 228
dark 94, 113, 168
dark and deep slumber 223
dark forces 168
dark moments 163
darkness 51, 56, 58, 59, 65,
    66, 70, 71, 83, 91,
    94, 95, 190
dead 97
dead human 201
death 143, 150, 200
decay and crumbling 219
deceived 85, 92, 181
decipher hidden codes 229
deep, dark valley 20
deeper level 54
deeper Love 176
deepest part of yourself 209
deepest parts of yourself 232
deity 149
deja vu 128
dense 227
dense earthly time frame 153
denser physical realities 226
denser physical reality 20
depression 40
descendant 102
descendants 137
designed for love 177
designed to survive 209
despair 211
despairing moments 209
destiny 66, 69, 84
destiny on Earth 89
destruction 79, 84, 85, 110
destruction of society 220
develop 180, 204

development 42, 62, 207, 211
Devil 16
die 187
differences 111
different belief systems 181
different dimensions. 231
different frequencies 175
different species 62
difficult journey 227
dimension 22, 60, 70, 76,
    156, 230
dimension of time 91
dimensional crossovers 229
dimensional focusing 151
dimensional realities 61
dimensional time 161
dimensions 59, 68, 97, 150,
    152, 203, 230
direct beam 81
disaster 110
disasters 85, 135
discernment 82, 92, 195
discoveries 197
dishearten 135
disheartened 71
disillusionment 117
divine 43, 113, 137, 222
divine connection 187
divine Creator 131, 149
divine deity 149
divine engineering, 27
divine hall of knowledge 186
divine intervention 27
divine law 82
divine love 173
divine music 77
divine nature 16, 142, 223
divine oneness 49
divine plan 131
divine purpose 29, 39, 159
divine purpose and plan 89
divine source 186

Index

Index

Index

Index

Index

Index

Index

Index

Index

Index

Index

Index

Index

Index

Index

Ordering This Book

Order through the Internet
www.starstreetpress.com
www.comestheawakening.com
www.lialight.com

Order through our 800 number
Call 1-800-587-9178

Order via mail
Star Street Press
420 7th Street NW
Suite 1013
Washington, DC 20004

If ordering by mail, please include the following order form (you can copy it onto your own paper). Your name must be the same as it appears on your credit card and the address and phone number must be the same as the credit card issuer shows for you. We do not accept checks. Shipping will be added to your order. In the United States "Comes The Awakening" is $23.95. For Canada, it is $35.50. If you are ordering from somewhere else, please call the 800 number or use the internet.

Number of copies

Name_____

Address_____

Address 2nd line_____

City_____State_____Zip_____

Phone number_____(in case of questions)

Credit card number_____

Expiration Date_____   Visa MC AMX Discover Diners

Signature_____Date_____

About the Author

L*ia* S*hapiro* spent a lifetime journeying down spiritual paths before she was ready to receive the messages contained in this book. During the *Hippy Revolution*, she was a flower child who started to awaken to her own truth. Later, she became a *Born Again Christian,* a spiritual state that lasted for thirteen years. Ultimately, while living in Japan, she *Awakened* to Pleiadian Energy. Interdimensional Contactee, Channeler, Writer, Speaker, Artist and Singer, Lia Shapiro brings new Pleiadian messages that will help to *Awaken, Transform, Evolve* and *In-Lighten* you.